"Leadership starts with restlessness: Something needs to be better. This book provides the compass and map to take the first steps and discover who you need to be to make that difference."
MICHAEL BUNGAY STANIER, bestselling author of *The Coaching Habit*

"Studio/E has a gift for helping high-integrity leaders discover new ways forward, even in the face of chaos and uncertainty. *Explore or Expire* provides not just new levels of awareness about what's possible in today's fast-shifting business realm, but also gratifying new pathways for getting there intact."
PILAR GERASIMO, founding editor of *Experience Life* magazine, cohost of *The Living Experiment* podcast, and author of *The Healthy Deviant*

"The art of exploration is the most effective approach to thriving in this rapidly changing world. *Explore or Expire* pushes individuals and teams to enter the unknown and emerge as more competent, creative, and generative humans."
CHERYL YAFFE KISER, executive director of the Institute for Social Innovation at Babson College and Babson Social Innovation Lab and coauthor of *Creating Social Value*

"*Explore or Expire* is a timely resource that everyone needs to successfully navigate toward the essentials for both themselves and their organizations. The principles in this book should be in every leader's tool kit to create a life that really matters, personally and professionally. It's in mine!"

ANDREW ZIMMERN, chef, television personality, writer, and global explorer

"Essentialists explore more than their nonessentialist counterparts. They create space for it. The rest of us get caught up in a Zoom-eat-sleep-repeat lifestyle. If you really want to break free from this and operate at your highest point of contribution, read and use this gem of a book."

GREG MCKEOWN, *New York Times*–bestselling author of *Effortless* and *Essentialism* and host of *The Greg McKeown Podcast*

"Unlocking the true potential of organizations hinges on retaining their intrapreneurs: the internal entrepreneurs who drive everyday innovation. *Explore or Expire* is a transformative guide that tackles this challenge head-on. The proven principles within nurture the confidence of intrapreneurs and empower leaders to cultivate an environment of autonomy, smart risk-taking, and passion, the very elements that create a road map to sustainable growth."

DR. SIMONE AHUJA, global innovation expert, keynote speaker, and bestselling author

"When I read *Explore or Expire*, I was reminded of three quotes from some of my Hero Teachers: 'What are you doing that makes your heart pitter-patter?' (Anne Bancroft); 'Adventure is an overused word; the adventure starts when something goes wrong' (Yvon Chouinard); and 'Encourage is the most important word in the world. Give courage' (Erik Weihenmayer). Read the book (you'll love it), participate in Studio/E (you'll be stretched), and enjoy the exploration."

JEFF PROUTY, chairman and founder of The Prouty Project

"Like me, you may fear having to deal with ambiguous situations because they cause you to feel stuck, hopeless, and alone. But thankfully for both of us, this book will empower you with the principles needed to courageously explore the unknown."

CORKY HALL, CEO of Stellus Consulting

"I had the pleasure of attending a Studio/E Expedition Program in person many years ago, and it positively impacted the way I think and act as a leader. Tom Wiese and Nate Garvis have bottled that magic into a book that's for anyone who's hungry to explore, launch new ideas, and navigate to a more desirable personal or professional future."

COREY CRISWELL, chief leadership officer at Adeption

"Several years ago, a client, a senior leader in a global airline company, made a statement that has informed my work ever since: 'I want to create a culture where I am excited to go to work and my people feel the same way.' In *Explore or Expire*, leaders are provided with the tools to do just that. The authors enable leaders to make a fundamental shift from seeing life as a struggle to perceiving life as an adventure. If you want to play it safe, this book is not for you; if you are playing to win, read, absorb, and implement every word."

DAVID MCNALLY, author of *Mark of an Eagle* and coauthor of *Be Your Own Brand*

"*Explore or Expire* is an essential resource for all of us facing the cascade of challenges and uncertainties that daily roil our times. It's not about just tweaking existing methods and systems—it is actively exploring, creating, and acting toward new possibilities. I've led organizations from federal and national to local and tiny, and I've never felt more energized, better equipped, and more in alignment than I have with the values, vision, resources, and methods in this book. Join Tom Wiese and Nate Garvis and others, and activate the explorer within—take the chance to thrive, to create, to lead."

DAVID O'FALLON, PhD, former CEO of the Minnesota Humanities Center

"The exploratory leadership principles and processes developed by Tom Wiese and Nate Garvis provide a common language and approach to explore the unknown and create new opportunities that help our customers, our associates, and our business to thrive. Since we engaged with Studio/E, the mindset and conversations in my company have changed. We are now building an army of exploratory leaders across all functions and at all levels of the organization. *Explore or Expire* puts forth a clear framework for exploration with practical, straightforward tools to guide you on your journey."

JOAN SCHATZ, CEO of Park Industries

"Tom Wiese and Nate Garvis have given the words 'explore' and 'navigate' new meaning. This second edition of *Explore or Expire* hones their keen perspectives to a sharper edge, giving us even better tools for our leadership journeys. Thank you, and onward!"

PETER BAILEY, president of The Prouty Project

"All leaders need to read this book. *Explore or Expire* takes proven leadership models and makes them approachable and practical. My team and I have worked with Studio/E for a few years, and I am a better leader because of their fresh way of helping leaders think, act, and inspire more purposefully."

DAVID MUCHA, head of strategy and innovation at Compeer Financial

EXPLORATORY LEADERSHIP PRINCIPLES FOR A RAPIDLY CHANGING WORLD

2ND EDITION

EXPLORE
or EXPIRE

Tom Wiese with Nate Garvis

PAGE TWO

Excerpt from Michael Bungay Stanier's "I'm Scarred,"
in *End Malaria: Bold Innovation, Limitless Generosity,
and the Opportunity to Save a Life*, pages 30–32, edited
by Michael Bungay Stanier (Domino Project, 2011),
is used with permission.

Cataloguing in publication information
is available from Library and Archives Canada.
ISBN 978-1-77458-426-2 (paperback)
ISBN 978-1-77458-427-9 (ebook)

Page Two
pagetwo.com

Edited by James Harbeck
Copyedited by Jenny Govier
Proofread by Alison Strobel
Cover, interior design, and illustrations by Fiona Lee
Tools and symbols originally designed by Jeff Johnson/Replace

exploreorexpirebook.com

CONTENTS

FOREWORD

STUDIO/E FOUNDERS Tom Wiese and Nate Garvis have created a method of leadership that works in any context. Their method is called Exploratory Leadership, and it takes us on a profound journey rooted in who we are, what we know, who we know, and, most importantly, what we desire.

Exploratory Leadership provides one of the most accessible and practical navigational tool sets for all of us who want to take that leap of faith to create the things we want in a world that is less knowable, more ambiguous, and definitely more uncertain than ever before.

What do you do when you are faced with the unknown? How do you find your goal—alone or within a team—when things are ambiguous and uncertain? How do you take your first step in the direction of your desires? Do you have what you need and who you need? If you had all you needed, what could be possible?

Exploratory Leadership asks us an important question: What is it we want to create? Then it artfully equips us with a map and the navigational tools to help us forge ahead and build a pathway to new possibilities.

Ignoring the ever-changing state of affairs isn't a wise option. We cannot merely manage our way forward. We have to explore, launch, and navigate with new tools. We need to see differently, think differently, and act differently. Our old habits won't get us there.

Tom and Nate have used decades of experience as entrepreneurs and corporate executives to craft a coherent, practical, and energy-producing method of leadership. They have beautifully woven their personal and professional insights and lived experiences into a coherent, practical, and invigorating leadership method.

Tom and Nate are also master explorers and have been on a journey for over a decade teaching thousands of leaders at Studio/E. The art of exploration is the most effective approach to thriving in this rapidly changing world.

Exploratory Leadership pushes individuals and teams to enter the unknown and emerge as more competent, creative, and generative humans. This approach, at its core, is one of optimism, joy, and the belief in what is possible. This leadership method will help you to make valuable discoveries, while influencing your team to come along on the journey.

CHERYL YAFFE KISER, *founding executive director, Institute for Social Innovation, Babson College, and Babson Social Innovation Lab; coauthor,* Creating Social Value: A Guide for Leaders and Change Makers

PREFACE TO
THE SECOND EDITION

THE FIRST EDITION of *Explore or Expire* was written during the COVID-19 pandemic (a time of great global uncertainty) to share the valuable principles that we learned to effectively navigate the unknown. These principles came from more than a decade of workshops with thousands of talented leaders learning to adopt Exploratory Leadership. The first edition was a cool-looking self-published textbook for our network. It was an experiment, or as we like to call it, an MVP (i.e., minimum viable progress). We produced a limited number of copies. We sold most of those copies to past participants and current participants of our programming. As our supply of the first edition dwindled, we were lucky enough to connect with a great publisher and book expert: Jesse Finkelstein at Page Two. Jesse liked the first edition of *Explore or Expire* and shared with us that her team could produce an engaging second edition that could be commercially available to everyone. Jesse and her team more than delivered on that promise.

The second edition of *Explore or Expire* has been revised and expanded with engaging stories of many exploratory leaders, past and present. The simple yet powerful principles and tools of Exploratory Leadership are used by these leaders on their everyday expeditions to successfully explore more possibility, launch new ideas, and navigate change in this rapidly changing world.

Welcome to your expedition!

INTRODUCTION
WE'VE BEEN TO
THE MOUNTAINTOP

Just like legendary explorers, entrepreneurs and intrapreneurs must navigate through unknown territories, pivot around unforeseen obstacles, and iterate toward their desired destination.

I N THE LOFTY tradition of Moses, Sir Edmund Hillary, and John Denver, we found our inspiration in the mountains. The Rocky Mountains, to be exact.

In Colorado on vacation on an early June morning in 2011, the air was crisp, the sky was blue, and our spouses were still asleep. We decided to go exploring and return in time for breakfast. Instead, we barely made it home for dinner because a realization stopped us in our tracks that inspired a day-long conversation: Many of our friends were not as happy as they should be, including us. Talented people with successful careers kept saying they were too frustrated, too stressed out, and, all too often, just plain stuck:

- The head of a major healthcare system touted some bold and crucial ideas, but the organization's leaders resisted them until they could be "proven." This inability to act caused the organization to miss opportunities to help its patients and stay relevant to its purpose.

- A C-suite executive at a Fortune 50 company lamented that her firm had lost its mojo. What was once a bulletproof corporation with amazing growth and a stellar reputation was now resting on its laurels, while the competition was beating it up and gaining ground.

* A CEO was surrounded by employees who had surrendered their souls to the hierarchical corporate culture. They kowtowed to the CEO's impressive title and never challenged themselves to think with originality. They only offered safe, perfectly formed ideas that could be flawlessly executed but failed to create any new value.

Some of our friends ran successful boutique organizations—for profit and nonprofit—but were blindsided by new technologies. They likewise overlooked rapidly changing consumer needs and novel business models that seemed to materialize overnight.

Many of our friends never executed their great ideas because they did not know how to navigate into the unknown. The well-being of our friends carried serious consequences. If these leaders and influencers could not move forward, the effects would be felt in their organizations, their communities, and their families.

Something had to be done!

The two of us have been friends since seventh grade, and we act like it—or so we are told. We grew up together in a Minneapolis suburb and helped each other survive our teenage years. After high school, we set out in different directions—to college and law school—and established separate, successful careers and networks. Now when we meet to talk and think, our combined perspectives give us a stereoscopic depth. We see things better together.

Standing on that mountain trail, we asked ourselves two simple questions:

Is there a common thread here?

What could we do to help?

We were no longer on a stroll. We were on a quest! We kept walking at the pace of a good chat. The hours flew by as we analyzed our friends' predicaments. Obviously, they were being stifled by the inability to initiate change in their organizations. It is typical for an organization to resist change, because somewhere along the way its actions become geared toward self-preservation, and any change becomes a threat to the status quo. Once this aversion to risk becomes institutionalized, rigor mortis sets in, and with it a lack of flexibility, agility, and foresight.

The problem wasn't bad people or a lack of talent. This was a problem of good and talented people operating in obsolete designs.

Versions of this same dilemma emerge everywhere and to everyone at some time, regardless of sector. It doesn't really matter whether you spend your professional life in business, government, nonprofits, medicine, the arts, or even a faith-based organization. At some point there is a tendency to turn your business model into your customer. We just keep feeding the machine and forget that the purpose of our product is to serve the needs of the customer—a living person who is constantly changing along with the rest of the universe. Rather than respond to the fluctuating needs of the users, institutionalized leaders remain fixed on doing what they've always done, because that is what worked in the past.

A textbook example of the sin of misplaced purpose is Kodak. This iconic producer of film and cameras dominated consumer photography since 1888. This market leader invented digital photography in the 1970s, and yet it went bankrupt in 2012. Why? In our exploratory opinion, Kodak misunderstood itself. Kodak thought of itself as a film business, when it was actually a company that enabled its customers to preserve their memories. It mistook the means for the end. For a hundred-plus years, film was the easiest way to preserve those memories. But the digital revolution changed that. Who needs to mess with cameras, film, and the expense of development when you have a smartphone? This story is a great lesson about understanding the difference between why you're in business and how you operate your business.

Fortunately, this is not the end of the story. We hear that Kodak has awakened from its institutional slumber and recalibrated its belief to one that can survive the unknown. Its new value statement states that "we believe in the power of technology and science to enhance what the world sees and creates."

Sadly, this classic shipwreck tale has become a common story for far too many organizations.

Thinking about this, we asked ourselves a few more questions about our stuck friends:

* What do our friends' clients really need? That's a difficult one to crack outside of the organization itself, because the answer really depends on their industry, desires, and opportunities.

* What value do their organizations actually provide? This is something that most companies try to test and retest, and they often come up with the right answer on their own.

⊛ Here's the hardest question to answer: Who does a great job of dealing with what is *actually emerging*, rather than just what is *predicted or expected*? As we looked out over the mountaintops, the answer became obvious: Explorers!

Successful entrepreneurs and intrapreneurs are the explorers of our age. Just like legendary explorers, entrepreneurs and intrapreneurs must navigate through unknown territories, pivot around unforeseen obstacles, and iterate toward their desired destination. Successful entrepreneurs and intrapreneurs do not go on endlessly planning for perfection; they take action. They *learn* their way forward.

We could best serve our friends by helping them acquire the exploratory skills that entrepreneurs and intrapreneurs use in their quests into the unknown.

Our final question: If we could equip leaders with the tools of exploration, entrepreneurship, and intrapreneurship, how could we create the most supportive and fertile learning environment?

Most leaders use their knowledge every day, but they often lack opportunities to add to that knowledge. When they do make it to a business seminar or workshop, it's usually filled with like-minded professionals in the same field as theirs. Alas, success over time engenders a tendency to narrow our thinking and restrict our social networks.

What if we could withdraw leaders from their insular circles and put them into a diverse space with successful leaders from other walks of life? Everyone becomes a student and a teacher to each other. If you really want to expand your knowledge, hang out with people who know things you don't.

At first we thought we should open an Ambiguity School to teach leaders how to find possibilities when they feel stuck. Throw away the old map that says you have reached a dead end, and see for yourself that the future is totally ambiguous—it could be anything!

Then we realized our friends didn't need a new school to merely enumerate options and gather information. What they needed was a place where they could learn to create new pathways forward from scratch—the exploratory principles that help leaders become more successful.

As we paused to take delight in the magnificence of the valley view that stretched below us, we resolved to establish a multidimensional exploratory learning community where our friends could safely learn to courageously explore, launch, and navigate ideas. This vision became Studio/E: Great Minds Navigating Change. More than a decade after our Colorado Rocky Mountain vision, Studio/E flourishes as an explorer training camp in the Upper Mississippi River Valley in Minnesota.

We returned many hours later, not weary, but energized by a vision for a new way to help our friends and colleagues navigate change and recalibrate their lifelong journeys in pursuit of meaningful prosperity.

Since that time, the Studio/E circle has grown to include thousands of exploratory leader graduates and fellow travelers. Dozens of Hero Teachers from across the world have inspired our collective consciousness with their insights, and, in this book, their paths offer insights into how to explore with ease. Like proud parents, we watch our exploratory leaders go forth into the unknown, pushing into new territories and navigating the unforeseen. Whether they launch startups or inject a dose of entrepreneurial spirit into their organizations, they blaze a trail that others can follow. We rejoice in awe of these fabulous and wise souls.

Through the magic of the written word, we've worked to distill the essence of our Studio/E experience into this book. Prepare to be provoked by a quest to stimulate and nourish the Exploratory Leadership Principles that are awakening within you. Be forewarned that we fully expect audience participation in this quest; armchair explorers will be left behind and stranded.

This book's purpose is to help you discover more possibility in your life through the concept of Exploratory Leadership. With more possibility, you can create the future you desire. We aim to outfit you with the principles—and their supporting lessons, questions, and practices—that you need to tackle the unknown. We will equip you to take *real* actions so that you can successfully *explore*, *launch*, and *navigate* through the perpetual change that engulfs us all.

There's what you plan for... and then there's what actually shows up.

We are honored to invite you to transform into that new version of yourself, where the future you desire is yours to create. Join us—and create more prosperity for yourself and those who rely on you.

Onward!

Expedition Map

REFLECTION

UNKNOWN

Navigate

STUDIO/E METHOD

Launch

POSSIBILITY

Explore

PREDICTION

AWARENESS & CHOICE

KNOWN

PART ONE

BASE CAMP

1

MOTIVATE

YOURSELF

Exploratory Leadership is the art of motivating people (including yourself) to effectively travel into the unknown with clarity and confidence to discover more possibility.

A S BUZZ ALDRIN, the second person to stand on the moon, once told us, "We explore or we expire."

Exploration is a process of discovery that is part of the essence of all animal life, including the human spirit. Exploration is a crucial component of our DNA because it enables us to survive.

Biologically, exploration always begins with the desire for continued existence. Our Paleolithic ancestors constantly explored for food, whether they were seeking edible plants and fruits or hunting animals to feast upon. Once people figured out how to grow their own food and raise their own livestock, our exploratory urge grew further. In search of new pathways, humans began to explore as a means of attaining all kinds of wealth: intellectual, cultural, and financial. We searched for trade routes, located oil for drilling, and launched whole new industries. Others sought knowledge, trying to figure out how the world worked by exploring the laws of motion and outer space. Still others sought ways to improve the human condition by exploring human physiology, diseases, and medicines.

As Jimmy Chin, mountaineering legend and Oscar-winning filmmaker, says, "As human beings, we have an innate need to explore, to see what's around the corner." Like a whole lot of folks you'll hear from in this book, Chin is one of our Hero Teachers, someone who has shown up at Studio/E to inspire us and share their wisdom.

All human modes of exploration have the same basic pattern of somehow moving from the known to the unknown, to provide value to the world. Exploratory leaders were the ones who figured out how to formulate their purpose into a plan of action, launch expeditions to places they had never been before, and navigate through unforeseen challenges.

What's our purpose? Purpose is our magnetic north—think of it as the basis for an exploratory leader's journeys into the unknown. Like the magnetic north that a compass needle points to in response to the earth's magnetic field, the exploratory leader's magnetic north points to a direction they should explore, driven by their own magnetic field, which is their purpose. And exploration is needed, personally and organizationally, because of the changes we are all experiencing and need to navigate.

Change has always been the norm, but in recent years the rate of change has accelerated. Market fluctuations and instability can be caused by everything from civil wars to trade wars, from changing tastes to new inventions, from chaotic climate events to pandemics that traverse the globe. The tsunami of the digital revolution caused widespread social and economic disruption. Entire industries were devastated, other sectors were transformed, and unforeseen industries emerged. The digital metamorphosis is accelerating with the growth of artificial intelligence and quantum computing. Combine those forces with globalism and other transformative technological advances, and all of a sudden the world is flat and connected. It's up to the exploratory leader to make sure we don't fall off the edge.

In our present-day world of work, we also know that the global marketplace is changing forever, and we're still seeking out ways to better the human condition. No one knows where we are headed, and the old ways of doing things aren't going to be good enough anymore. We need the skills and vision of a new kind of leadership. Each one of us needs to become an exploratory leader.

Exploratory Leadership is the art of motivating people (including yourself) to effectively travel into the unknown with clarity and confidence to discover more possibility.

Exploratory leaders excel in moving forward in the face of uncertainty. They navigate through volatile, uncertain, complex, and ambiguous conditions while generating a new kind of clarity and inspiring motivation and confidence. They shape their environment as they explore the unknown, finding value for their teams by launching and navigating according to a new set of ideas.

That's why a key part of Exploratory Leadership is inspiring others to buy into your vision, whether they be your crew, your investors, or your CFO. The conventional habits of business-as-usual, while important, can create a fear of the unknown and an avoidance of the unpredictable. The exploratory leader must reawaken in others their latent explorer instinct. The marketplace—and your survival in that marketplace—depends on it.

But leadership travels in a number of different directions. Our continued existence depends not just on how each one of us adapts but also on how we all adapt as a community. Success depends upon inspiring everyone on board to go along for the ride. We humans are hard-wired to be uncomfortable with anything new, which is a big reason efforts to facilitate organizational and personal change fail so often.

"All the important things in life," Olympic gold medal winner Jessie Diggins shared with us, "we don't achieve totally by ourselves, even though sometimes it looks that way. You might get up on the podium by yourself, but there's this huge crowd of people that lifted you up there through teamwork."

She's right. We exist to motivate each other.

"When you join a team," Diggins explains, "you say, all right, I'm committing to this thing that is bigger than just me. And so by having this group ownership of any success, we transform it into a team endeavor."

The world is constantly changing, yet many people act as though this isn't true. Most people settle into the traditional habits of life, society, and business and find comfort in the familiar.

But you aren't like most people, are you?

Exploratory leaders uproot traditional habits because they know they must adapt to the changing world to ensure the viability of their enterprises—and the vitality of all of us. Exploration is essential to thriving in our rapidly changing world. It's one thing to be proficient with a conventional mindset to maintain the status quo, but one must transcend the predictable world and adopt a new, unconventional mentality to find more possibility.

The best future is the one we create, not one that happens to us.

2

CREATE A
NEW
FUTURE

Rather than being trapped by the status quo, **exploratory leaders embrace principles that generate motivation, clarity, and confidence to design a new future.**

"DECISION MAKERS at the *New York Times* used to sit around a King Arthur–style round table to decide on the six stories that would go on the first page of the newspaper every day," author and TED speaker Priya Parker once told us.

The editors would come with their offerings to the publishers and editor-in-chief, and those decision makers would determine what the city's, or even the country's, populace would talk about that day. And so this daily meeting was really important. It became a hallowed event. It became a ritual.

"Right now, however, our companies have ritualized meetings that have lost meaning, because they no longer serve the present purpose," Parker says when she teaches leaders and communities how to have complicated conversations during times of transition.

Because, following the newspaper example further, now there's this thing called the homepage, with hundreds of stories a day on that one page. What goes on a news site homepage is often decided by an algorithm. And the majority of readers don't even come to that homepage. They access news stories through social media.

What does that mean? It means that this particular ritual is no longer relevant.

Parker further explained, "I would make a distinction between routine and ritual. One of the best definitions of ritual that I've seen is [from] Jonathan Cook, who's an ethnographer. He defines it very simply as something we do over and over again to which we ascribe meaning. And that meaning can be transformational."

When the meaning stops being, well, meaningful, something has to shift. An exploratory leader is adept at realizing how things could be different and creating new meaning in what we do together, so that our actions can facilitate change. Such a visionary sees beyond the here and now and imagines new possibilities, new options, and new approaches. Exploratory leaders are always on the lookout for new possibilities, and they also keep an eye out for how they, and their organizations, need to change to continue serving their purpose, whether it is responding to oncoming challenges or proactively discovering new directions.

In fact, as Abraham Lincoln and others have said, "The best way to predict the future is to create it."

Feel the Change You Want to See

Having a future-oriented vision is just the first step.

When humans lived in caves, unforeseen dangers killed us all the time. And our brains are still wired to respond to that constant state of threat. Even in uncomfortable conditions, the attitude of the rank and file is "better the devil we know than the devil we don't."

In fact, many individuals report a strong sense of discomfort with their uncertainty of where they actually are, and they may ignore the signals they are receiving from the world around them. For example, often when we are in the unknown, we feel physical anguish. Or we may be in denial, falsely maintaining that we are in the known so as to avoid any unpleasant feelings. That awareness of our physical sensations is important information. The body is always in the present, so listen to it! Mind and body awareness allow us to sense what is going on.

Our biology reacts with amazing rapidity when it senses the unknown, as Dr. Terry Wu has explained to us. That awareness puts us in a position to correctly choose which tools to use. Wu teaches about the primordial survival mechanism centered in the brain's limbic system, which is driven by the amygdala. The amygdala is always on the alert for threats to our safety. Before we can even think, it can sound the alarm, triggering our fight/flight/freeze response. Its responses are based on past experience, so when anything new enters the picture, it elicits immediate suspicion, and we become uneasy. If the amygdala judges it to be a major threat, then our response is to be deathly afraid of the unknown.

One flaw in the design of the amygdala is that it cannot distinguish whether we are facing an actual threat to our life or just watching a movie. It sounds the alarm and triggers a shot of adrenalin just the same. If it were consistent, it would also be dreadfully afraid of the future, but the amygdala can be fooled there too. For example, the global calendar system reduces our fear of the unknown because we can look at any future date and identify it by name—yes, that's Wednesday, November 10, 2060. These characteristics of a calendar are hallmarks of predictability. And then there is a horde of fortune tellers to assuage our fears—market analysts, futurists, and astrologers. They make a good living simulating predictability, and the amygdala doesn't know the difference.

But we explorers have biology on our side too.

It is in the DNA of all animals to take intentional actions into the unknown. Our survival depends on confronting challenges, learning new things, and creating change. The explorer part of us is rewarded by the hippocampus, another a part of our brain associated with the limbic system. The hippocampus rewards curiosity with a shot of dopamine; this part of the brain handles our memories, old and new, and it is always glad to learn something. It rewards explorations that bring new knowledge.

Too often we ignore the important physical signals of the unknown and pretend to ourselves that we know what we're looking at. That lie results in going back to our tried-and-true, predictive behaviors. And that can be reckless in the unknown. But recklessness can be avoided. Exploration is an activity, so the more we practice, the less likely we are to engage in this kind of unproductive denial of what is actually in front of us.

The fear that any change could bring something worse results in people clinging to the status quo as if it were a security blanket. The exploratory leader knows that the stability of the status quo is an illusion. Rather than being trapped by the status quo, they embrace principles that generate motivation, clarity, and confidence to design a new future. Every business operation is provisional; it must be transformed when conditions warrant.

The former chairman of advertising firm Saatchi & Saatchi, Kevin Roberts, says in his marvelous book *64 Shots: Leadership in a Crazy World* that the future is ultra-turbulent. "We live in a VUCA world. Volatile. Uncertain. Complex. Ambiguous. VUCA is a military acronym that has penetrated business speak. It recognizes that running a business has become like flying through an asteroid field."

How is it possible to navigate through a storm of cosmic turbulence that can render obsolete everything we know? Old-fashioned planning doesn't work because the VUCA universe is unpredictable.

Or, to quote from *The Avengers*, from the Marvel Universe:

Captain America: "We need a plan of attack!"

Iron Man: "I have a plan. Attack."

Likewise, the exploratory leader must act without a plan. No plan survives in a VUCA world. Quite simply, exploratory leaders *explore* first, *launch* ideas, and *navigate* based on what is discovered.

Another vast sector involves the unpredictable and turbulent changes in human capital and how they manifest as generational transformation, which never stops changing. Witness the emergence in the job market of Gen Z (born 1995–2012). According to father/son

Gen Z experts David and Jonah Stillman (guess which one is a Gen Z), the incoming generation carried with it a new set of expectations for their desired workplace environments.

For example, having been weaned on social media and smartphones, Gen Zers have conflated physical reality with digital reality to form a "phigital" mindset. The two worlds are virtually indistinguishable. Their egos demand hyper-customization, but their social sensitivities embrace shared business models—"weconomics."

The VUCA world is very unstable and fluid because of the accelerating pace of change and disruption. People are either too busy or too distracted to pay any attention to it. When the water is constantly warming up, people ignore it until it starts boiling. That's why we need exploratory leaders. They have the vision to see things beyond the current state.

Exploratory leaders possess a vivid sense of possibility, and they create more possibility for themselves and those around them. Their big-picture perspective includes an understanding of why people have trouble seeing beyond what they know. At the same time, they know how to persuade people to join in their expeditions into the unknown.

The time to create the future, rather than merely react to it, is *now*.

3

TAKE YOUR
FIRST STEPS

INTO THE
UNKNOWN

In the unknown world, the mind goes into exploratory mode, and **its logic is expressed in the form of a question: What if?**

WHAT IF? Imagine, if you will, that the known and the unknown are two entirely different dimensions. Like parallel universes, they can occupy the same spot, but they vibrate at totally different frequencies. These two dimensions operate in different ways. They each require different mindsets, different competencies, different methods, and different behaviors to successfully navigate and execute. They also have different characteristics and generate different outcomes. They require you to be dually literate.

But most importantly, they operate according to different logics.

In the known world, cognition is geared toward prediction and uses the standard logical inference structure: **If, then.**

In the unknown world, the mind goes into exploratory mode, and its logic is expressed in the form of a question: **What if?**

A major challenge to becoming an exploratory leader is learning to be aware of whenever you are in the known and whenever you are in the unknown. The Realm of the Known is the world of prediction: What has worked in the past will work again. The Realm of the Unknown is the world of possibility: You don't know yet what will work.

The Realm of the Known

The known world is the land of business-as-usual, a closed system wherein everything has already been mapped and conventional wisdom reigns. In the Realm of the Known, a quantified analysis of the past endorses tried-and-true methods, so you can safely invest in things with a predictably high return. Change is not on the agenda, except for growth in scale, profits, efficiency, and market share. It is a linear land of conformity, regularity, and best practices, which gives rise to big plans once you have all your ducks in a row. Your rationale for the plan crunches all the known data and has all the answers to any objections—so you avoid risk and always aim for a sure thing.

That's why we call this world the Zone of Prediction. Business processes that don't account for the kind of rapid changes we're facing right now are those that try to predict the future—and fail.

We're in the Zone of Prediction because that's what we're used to. Virtually everybody dwells in the known world nearly all of the time, and anyone who has worked in an established organization, or has gone to school, is quite familiar with it. It's our status quo. Patterns of behavior are regular to the point of forming habits and fostering absent-mindedness. What typically happens is that we become immersed in our work and never question the superstructure. After work, we watch TV or look at our phone or seek other non-exploratory activities.

Make no mistake: The known world is the fragile foundation of modern civilization, and there's a lot of it we can still use every day. It is extremely important to respect the value of putting knowledge under our belt and retrieving it without having to reinvent it. The known world provides stability and comfort to our way of life.

But remain wary; if overdone, it can work against you. Don't let predictability lure you into lethargy. If you let down your guard, you surely will miss the signs of looming change.

That's because the closed system of the known world contains a fatal flaw: It is not sustainable. The known world is a human construction. We made it up so we could have things work in comforting predictability. However, it is not built to handle unforeseen changes. The unknown is like power-sucking kryptonite to our human-constructed known world.

In order to respond to the accelerating changes in the world, we have to venture into the Realm of the Unknown, and that requires the mindset of an exploratory leader.

Exploratory leaders know that creating value is a synthesis of two crucial elements: being *responsive* to the needs of users, and being *relevant* to the needs of users. We can control responsiveness, but we cannot control what is relevant to our users. The challenge is that our users' definition of relevance is constantly changing. It is precisely for that reason that we all need to be constantly exploring newly relevant ideas as well.

The Realm of the Unknown

What's important to note about the unknown world is that it hasn't been fully mapped. The Realm of the Unknown doesn't yet have lines indicating shores and valleys, mountains and streams. We have to create our own map, one step at a time, by exploring. Think of it as a mental model. We cannot predict what we will find after that first step, but we know we will surely learn something from it. We may only learn that we are going in the wrong direction, but even that bit of acquired knowledge adds clarity and helps to plan for the next step in our quest.

The exploratory leader always seeks new possibilities while simultaneously running their organizations. Often that means setting out in unexplored areas, but it can also mean seeing the known world through new lenses.

To view the here and now in a new way, we can take all the laws, plans, and best practices, and then turn them upside down and shake them—like erasing an Etch A Sketch. On that blank slate, you can recast the world in a new light.

In our minds we imagine a map of the world that rests upon our assumptions. Many of those assumptions are based on ensuring continued survival, not on thriving by exploring new possibilities. Our mental map is something we create for ourselves. That means that we can just as simply invent a new map. And in this map? We're now talking about adding the Zone of Possibility.

Here's what we mean: There's a big difference between the realms of the known and the unknown when it comes to what is possible. There is a world of possibility in which we can chart a new course where we can thrive in new ways. This is what the characteristics of the two realms look like:

Characteristics of the Realms

Realm of the Known (Zone of Prediction)	Realm of the Unknown (Zone of Possibility)
Big planning (Requires big assumptions)	**Small actions** (Allows for easy, affordable steps, requiring fewer assumptions)
Waiting till we get what we need	Starting with what we have
Expecting a return on investment	Knowing that our return is not immediate
Traveling in a linear direction	Traveling iteratively
Avoiding failure	Embracing learning
Acting competitively	Working collaboratively
Demanding answers	Asking questions

To successfully navigate change, we need to grow beyond merely managing an operation and take actions that lead exploratory expeditions of discovery into the unknown to find new relevance, learning, and possibility. Our resistance to change is overcome by our passionate curiosity to know what is around the next bend, what is new, what is next. Instead of competing with other companies in our market, we are trailblazing toward something unique—an "only" in a sector of reality where no one has gone before. And the outcomes in the Realm of the Unknown are generative and valuable, but perhaps different than what we've valued in the past.

Outcomes of the Realms

Realm of the Known (Zone of Prediction)	Realm of the Unknown (Zone of Possibility)
Scale	Agility
Execution	Learning
Responsiveness	Relevance
Optimization	Experimentation
Win/lose	Possibility

Why do these new outcomes matter?

We need to rise, building on our knowledge and through our own actions, and become an accelerating force for social change. We also need to step up and create the future we want if we want to ensure a positive future for our businesses, one that can navigate those icebergs rather than go down with the ship. If the goal is to be future-proof, we've got to jump the divide between the status quo and the possible.

Even though the known world tends to be self-satisfied, it can always use new knowledge—and that's what explorers provide! Every expedition into the unknown results in a discovery, one that sheds light on a new corner of our universe. By revealing new knowledge to the world, exploration provides clarity where once there was darkness.

As we move from the Realm of the Known to the Realm of the Unknown, we move from managerial tools and ideas to exploratory tools and ideas.

To take action to explore, launch, and navigate the unknown, you're going to have to shift the tools you use (your mindset, competency, and method) away from the known to the unknown. Here's what that looks like:

Realm of the Known (Zone of Prediction)	Tools	Realm of the Unknown (Zone of Possibility)
Manager	✳ Mindset	Explorer
Produce answers	∞ Competency	Ask questions
Plans and data	🔺 Method	Action

 Our **mindset** is the lens through which we see the world, and it has a great effect on how we perceive and act on what is in front of us. The exploratory leader's mindset is one that is open to possibility and driven by curiosity and purpose.

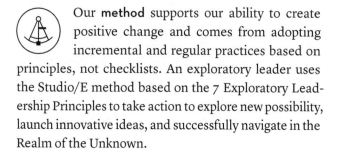

Building our **competency** allows us to create lasting change by doing something successfully or efficiently. An exploratory leader masters the competency of asking questions to discover new possibility.

Our **method** supports our ability to create positive change and comes from adopting incremental and regular practices based on principles, not checklists. An exploratory leader uses the Studio/E method based on the 7 Exploratory Leadership Principles to take action to explore new possibility, launch innovative ideas, and successfully navigate in the Realm of the Unknown.

Why not invent a new route to discover relevance, generative ideas, and possibility?

4

MAP

YOUR WAY

If we buckle up and explore the unknown, we discover more possibilities for new relevance and transformation. **More possibilities mean more opportunities.**

ERE'S WHAT Jimmy Chin once shared with us: "When you're in an unknown situation," he said, "your first job is to find clarity and focus and build from there. Composure, rather than panic—that's the one thing that's going to serve you."

Many great stories begin with a map to provide a visual depiction of the adventure ahead. That's why, to guide your initial foray into exploration, Studio/E invented an allegorical map we call the Expedition Map that helps you to get a handle on both the known *and* the unknown. An allegorical map portrays worlds and regions of the mind, rather than the geography of the physical. The Expedition Map is shown on the following page (and also in Appendix A). As you move into and through Part Two of this book, we will explain the elements of the Expedition Map in greater detail. The Expedition Map will guide you with a visual, spatial sense of where you are, where you have been, and what actions you need to take.

Expedition Map

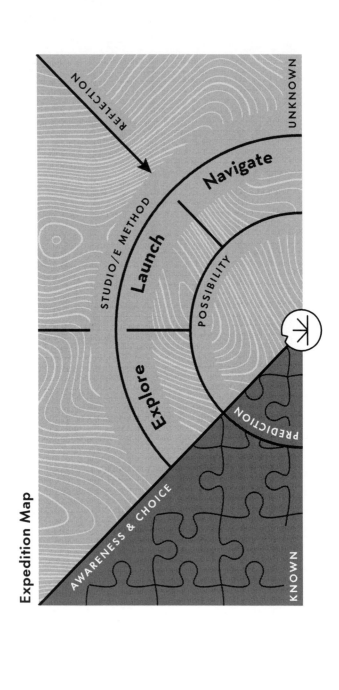

REFLECTION

UNKNOWN

Navigate

STUDIO/E METHOD

Launch

POSSIBILITY

Explore

PREDICTION

AWARENESS & CHOICE

KNOWN

The Expedition Map incorporates the elements of Exploratory Leadership in the features described below:

 The **puzzle pieces** signify what we know already and our managerial mindset. They indicate the Realm of the Known (Zone of Prediction) on the map.

 The **topographical lines** signify the unknown and our exploratory mindset. They indicate the Realm of the Unknown (Zone of Possibility) on the map.

 The **notched compass** is our symbol for the Studio/E Method of Exploratory Leadership. The notch on the compass points to the magnetic north we all have: our purpose. The lines, like an open book, symbolize the power of possibility. Your purpose and the possibility it can create is the element that makes the Expedition Map uniquely yours. That's why we put the notched compass on the spine of the book and at a pivotal place on the Expedition Map. Stay true to your overarching purpose, as you can only thrive over the long term when you are aligned with it. We will unlock your purpose in Part Two of this book.

Between the Realm of the Known and the Realm of the Unknown, there is a line representing **awareness and choice**. When you know which realm you are in, you can simply choose the correct tools to use, actions to take, and traits to embrace. For example, when launching an idea you know how to execute, you would use the known-realm tools (have the mindset of a manager; seek answers first; use plans and data). If you are trying to explore for new ideas or launch ideas that you don't know how to execute, then you would use the unknown-realm tools (have the mindset of an explorer; ask questions; take action). The remainder of this book is about exploring the unknown for new ideas and launching new ideas you don't know how to execute or navigate.

Within the Realm of the Unknown on the Expedition Map, there are three sections that contain the 7 Exploratory Leadership Principles:

- **Explore** in alignment with your purpose.

- **Launch** using a curious explorer's mindset within an exploratory learning community.

- **Navigate** with packaged idea MVPs, exploratory questions, declared action, and reflection.

These Exploratory Leadership Principles guide you to take action to explore new possibility, launch innovative ideas, and successfully navigate in the Realm of the Unknown.

The final element of the Expedition Map is the **reflection line** in the Realm of the Unknown. This is a reminder to stop and reflect on what you are learning so that you can make adjustments and pivot toward the future action you will take to reach your goal and plant your flag.

Warning: Before You Use Your Expedition Map

Remember, all of us have found comfort in familiar things. Wanting to feel safe and avoid what's new and different persists now just as it ever has, but it doesn't exactly ensure survival on contemporary planet Earth. Our world is constantly throwing new things at us. Yes, there was a time when it was safe to think that new equaled danger. But now, staying in the cave is dangerous. The safety of the status quo is the new danger.

ADVISORY: CAUTION!

We have worked with many organizations that seek innovation and want to explore and create learning cultures for the Realm of the Unknown. Often we discover that the company's ideas, metrics, and rewards are tailored solely for the Realm of the Known. Consequently, there is no incentive to go into the Realm of the Unknown to explore, and often employees will get unintentionally punished for doing so. The solution for this is to make sure to develop ideas, metrics, and rewards for both realms, with buy-in from stakeholders, and to share those items with your organization. Be mindful that typical ideas from the Realm of the Known that everyone so readily accepts were invented by someone in the past from the Realm of the Unknown. So go ahead, discover something new.

But we can shift out of the quicksand of the status quo. Practice doesn't make perfect; it creates comfort in the unknown.

Get comfortable with the discomfort of Exploratory Leadership and you'll be able to seamlessly flow back and forth between the realms of the known and unknown like a jazz artist or a jam band. Conquer your amygdala or it will control you. It's a scary prospect to suddenly doubt whether everything we know is actually true. Psychologists say that when our ideas are seriously challenged, we suffer from cognitive dissonance. When the mind is in gridlock, we react through our emotions and our bodies. We get angry and defensive, our stomach hurts, and our palms get sweaty. Does it feel hot in here? Like any shift in the human experience, it takes some time to go from denial to acceptance, and it's not a sure thing.

You should expect that the same feelings and physical symptoms will arise as you embark upon journeys into the unknown. Remember, that's just your biology talking to you. Listen to it so you can put yourself into a proper sense of awareness to choose the right mindset, tools, and traits. It will calm you down!

Start with Awareness of Your Traits on the Expedition Map

It helps to engage in exercises that develop exploratory awareness about the behavioral traits to embrace on the Expedition Map. Let's try an awareness exercise that will help you calmly learn to leave your old map behind and start exploring with your new Expedition Map. Then you'll be able to set forth optimistically with a blank slate, like a new notebook on the first day of school—filled with nothing but endless possibilities.

Understanding where you are comfortable can point you toward where you can better grow your experience.

Look at this table:

A (Managerial)	B (Exploratory)
Answers	Questions
Titles	First names
Organization structure	Alignment
Assumptions	Curiosity
Comparisons	Personal standards
Urgency	Values
Competition	Collaboration

How comfortable do you feel with the traits in columns A and B? Which column is a closer fit to your current way of being (think percentages; for example, 70 percent column A/30 percent column B)? Where are you more comfortable?

Can you think of times when you exemplified the traits from either column? Where do your heroes fit in these columns?

Remember, this is an awareness exercise, not a judgment exercise. We have all experienced different percentages of the A (managerial) and B (exploratory) traits. The important thing is to be aware of which traits you are leaning on and using at any point in time.

We need more column B (exploratory) traits when exploring the unknown. The world is vast and mysterious. For the most part, we don't know what we don't know. We carve out a tiny corner to inhabit and pretend that this known world is all there is. It's like playing a game, and we become totally immersed. We ignore all the doubt about the uncertainties and cling to the familiar. This is not sustainable because it excludes the inevitability of change.

However, if we buckle up and explore the unknown, we discover more possibilities for new relevance and transformation. More possibilities mean more opportunities. New possibility lies in the unknown.

Being dually literate in both managerial and exploratory principles allows us to execute in the known while exploring new ways to discover value in the unknown. Get ready to *explore*, *launch*, and *navigate* the unknown.

PART TWO

EXPLORE, LAUNCH, AND NAVIGATE

5

FIND
YOUR
INSPIRATION

Principles are primary truths for effectively dealing with certain situations or challenges in life.

ONE OF our honorary (and posthumous) Studio/E Hero Teachers is Anglo-Irish polar explorer Ernest Shackleton, a principal figure of the period known as the Heroic Age of Antarctic Exploration.

During the Heroic Age of Antarctic Exploration (1897–1922), Antarctica became the focus of many international expeditions launched for scientific discovery, geographic mapping, and study of the mysterious continent. A common issue with these expeditions was a lack of proper equipment to navigate the extreme environment and the inability to communicate with the outside world. Many of these expeditions became feats of great endurance by their personnel that sometimes exceeded their physical and mental limits. At the young age of twenty-seven, Shackleton made his first trip to the continent as the third officer of Captain Robert Falcon Scott's *Discovery* expedition in 1901, and in 1907 he returned for the first time to lead his own crew on the *Nimrod* expedition, aiming to be the first to trek to the South Pole and South Magnetic Pole. Under extreme weather conditions, Shackleton and a small party made it to the South Magnetic Pole, but, approximately 97 miles short of the South Pole, they had to turn back due to a lack of food. Shackleton's deep desire to be an explorer always had with it a boundary of protecting human life. After he turned back, so close to the South Pole, he wrote to his wife, Emily, "I thought, dear, that you would rather have a live ass than a dead lion."

Shackleton's third and largest expedition, the one that we'll be highlighting in this book, began in 1914 as his crew set sail from a small whaling station on South Georgia Island with the goal of the first human crossing of Antarctica from the Weddell Sea via the South Pole to the Ross Sea. Soon after its start, the Imperial Trans-Antarctic Expedition was mired by challenge after challenge. Off the shore of Antarctica, the expedition ran into thick sea ice while trying to make its initial landing. For weeks the crew navigated around these ice floes until they were eventually surrounded by thickening ice. Ultimately, the expedition's ship, the *Endurance*, was stuck, frozen in a massive block of ice within a hundred miles of the Antarctic shore on January 18, 1915.

Over the next ten months, the expanding ice rotated outwards, gradually crushing and ultimately sinking the *Endurance* on November 21, 1915. The crew floated hundreds of miles away from the continent and toward the South Sea. Shackleton was responsible for not only his own life but the lives of his crew of twenty-seven. Death seemed imminent as they sat on a melting ice floe headed into the most violent sea in the world. There was no instruction book for this expedition into the unknown. For more than twenty months, Shackleton and his crew faced unknowable crises again and again. He repeatedly navigated through a series of disasters that by all accounts should have brought certain death. If this story had not been so well documented in the diaries of the crew and the photographs of Frank Hurley, it would be easy to believe this epic tale was pure Hollywood fiction, fabricated for a summer blockbuster.

Following Shackleton's Path

Ernest Shackleton was fluent in both managing the known world and exploring the unknown.

That's why his story is going to help us traverse our own journey to Exploratory Leadership. There are many different Hero Teachers you'll also read about in the next few chapters, but this expeditioner's work provides us with a clear problem to solve and an outcome that matters. Shackleton and his diversely skilled crew successfully overcame life-or-death events by using the same principles we employ in this book, principles inspired by his leadership decisions. Principles are primary truths for effectively dealing with certain situations or challenges in life. If you embrace them, you don't need to exert the same amount of energy each time you encounter certain situations or challenges, and they yield valuable outcomes. The 7 Exploratory Leadership Principles that follow will help you successfully explore possibility, launch new ideas, and navigate change when you are in the unknown.

A Note of Caution

Mapping your path ahead will result in the formation of a new lens on life, and it may result in periodic frustration with conventional wisdom. Extensive practice will heighten your sense of purpose and relevance. Mastering Exploratory Leadership may at times involve irritation when you are confronted by resisters to change.

But you need not be anxious at the thought of changing your entire life. That won't be necessary. In fact, there's no need to toss away all of your own terrific principles that have led you to your current state of greatness. Think of what lies ahead as *additional* principles, not *replacement* principles. We've found that if we devote as little as 10 percent of our time to harnessing curiosity through Exploratory Leadership, we will create profound and valuable pathways to go forth and create a more prosperous future. This is an "and," not an "or."

Congratulations as you embark on your expedition to become an exploratory leader! These transformative principles have the power to alter the course of your life and the lives of those you influence and lead. These skills will equip you to explore the unknown, find new possibilities, and change the future for all. This responsibility requires an adventurous spirit, an open mind, and the courage to keep going in the face of uncertainty.

What lies ahead is like an entrepreneurial quest—we're going to point out the milestones you'll need to seek out, and you can join in as soon as you're ready. We have provided a logbook at the end of each Exploratory

Leadership Principle with a question prompt, so you can fully embrace what you have learned, and a practice you can apply to your expeditions into the unknown. In Part Three, we introduce you to the Expedition Action Compass, combining all the principles, that will advise you on which actions to take to successfully explore, launch, and navigate your ongoing expeditions in the unknown. These tools are also provided in a worksheet in Appendix B.

By adopting these principles, you'll be able to start exploring on your own to create a more prosperous future. It's time to become an exploratory leader.

6

EXPLORE

YOUR

PURPOSE

Purpose is greater than any one idea, and you can generate as many ideas as you want as you navigate your purpose into reality.

A FTER THE *Endurance* became frozen fast in an ice floe, Shackleton knew he had to make some key, on-the-spot decisions that redefined the goal—not the purpose—of his expedition.

When the *Endurance* sank, his goal shifted from being the first to trek across the continent to bringing everyone home alive.

In the very short term, he knew he had to create a micro-known world for the comfort of his crew while they tried to find solutions to free the ship. In the midst of an unbelievable situation, he set up an ordered regimen of activities and duties for his crew to test a range of options. By keeping everyone busy, he took their minds off the total insanity of their predicament and assumed a relative sense of normalcy as they continued to explore, using the best of their scientific skills.

Shackleton was gliding between the known and the unknown.

Purpose is greater than any one idea (or goal), and you can generate as many ideas as you want as you navigate your purpose into reality. Accordingly, when the expedition ultimately failed to reach their highly publicized goal of trekking across Antarctica, Shackleton did not wallow in the fact for long. Instead, he adopted a new goal of getting all his crew home alive. Shackleton's purpose was to explore for fame, fortune, and scientific discovery, but not at the cost of human life.

Like Shackleton, great exploratory leaders fall in love with their purpose, not their ideas.

In the unknown world, purpose is recognized as the springboard for all action, the source of profound energy, and the origin of why we matter. Our fundamental purpose is to live a life of meaning that keeps us going, and it is our heart's purpose that lights up our pathway through life.

While profitability is important, it alone is incomplete. Exploratory leaders pursue prosperity *and* possibility— profitability and so much more. Thankfully, a growing body of research points to the same conclusion: There is great utility and return in being grounded in purpose.

Aristotle wrote that everyone desires happiness, so the purpose of life is to pursue happiness. The problem is that people disagree on the nature of happiness and how to get there. Some seek material wealth. Many equate happiness with pleasure. Others go for honor and fame. Aristotle dismissed those notions and concluded that happiness is a lifetime of activity that we take to fulfill our highest potential. Happiness depends on what we find within ourselves, and nothing else.

Your heart's desire, when expressed through a lifetime of action, unlocks your purpose and gives life meaning. If you look at your life as a whole, following your true purpose will fulfill your destiny and establish your legacy.

Exploratory Principle 1:
Explore in Alignment with Your Purpose

Having a strong purpose gives impetus to the action you take. It is the underlying reason why you do things that matter to you. Purpose creates energy and resilience and serves as a filter so you can focus on the essentials during expeditions into the unknown.

Your purpose determines what is important to you. We don't *create* our purpose, we *unlock* it, says bestselling author Richard Leider. We all have a purpose waiting to emerge. Once you discover your purpose, you can activate it. When it is activated, it shows up in what you do in your daily life and produces motivation.

Imagine how people with different purposes might approach a mountain. Someone whose purpose is to bring visual beauty to the world (such as an artist) would notice its shape and texture and how the colors appear at different times of day. Someone whose purpose is to construct safely built environments might judge the size and variety of the trees and where might be a good place for a road. Someone whose purpose is to explore might look at pathways to the summit. Our purpose highlights the elements in the world that are the most relevant because they give us meaning and motivate us into taking action. If what lies in front of us is merely interesting but doesn't spark immediate energy inside, perhaps the best choice is to pass.

Articulating your purpose fixes your magnetic north in life, which guides your decisions, helps you steer around obstacles, and gives you the courage to face challenges. Your dedication to purpose also prevents you from getting sidetracked by mistaking your "how" for the "why"—like mistaking the means for the end.

As a young child, Hero Teacher John O'Leary survived burns to 100 percent of his body. He almost died in the process, but he went on to become a worldwide thought leader. O'Leary told us how he used purpose to navigate his way through this nearly impossible situation by sharing his favorite quote, inspired by Viktor Frankl and Friedrich Nietzsche: "When you know your why, you can endure any how." It's like Simon Sinek explains: "Why" is probably the most important message that an organization or individual can communicate, as this is what inspires others to action. Knowing your purpose directs you to where you should explore and provides you with the energy to do so.

That's how your purpose filters out what is not important and highlights what really matters.

Fueling Up

When the *Endurance* got stuck in the ice, Shackleton and his crew soon recognized their predicament. They weren't able to shift the hull out of the ice, and as January turned to February, they realized they'd have to hold out until Antarctica's spring in September before anything could be accomplished.

The ship drifted northward, and everyone turned to each other to get through the many months of isolation.

Soon, the crew members were playing soccer on the ice and singing along with a banjo to entertain themselves and the penguins, always having assigned roles and responsibilities and taking comfort in the occasional cup of grog, although Shackleton preferred aged Scotch whisky. He knew that maintaining the morale of the crew was essential for survival, so he always displayed an optimistic and hopeful attitude, along with the reliable certainty that he was in charge. He provided clarity in an uncertain situation, an example of his mastery of dual literacy in connecting to the known while in the unknown.

Our purpose provides a vast reservoir of energy to fuel and sustain our authentic actions, along with courage, resilience, and determination. These qualities give us the strength and motivation to follow our unique path into the unknown.

Our legacy as an exploratory leader will be the influence we had on other people and our community, and how we inspired them and showed them unforeseen possibilities. Those who benefit from our legacy will define the meaning and purpose of our life in terms of that legacy. The list of positions, degrees, and accomplishments on our résumé are notable manifestations of our purpose, but they don't constitute our purpose. Whenever we find ourselves lost, stuck, or confused, we must revisit our purpose, let it guide us back to our path, and refuel for the road ahead.

EXPLORE IN ALIGNMENT WITH YOUR PURPOSE

Lesson

Purpose creates energy and resilience, and it serves as a filter so you can focus on the essentials during expeditions into the unknown. Remember, when your purpose is activated, it produces motivation.

Question

What is your purpose, and are you aligned with it?

_____

_____

_____

_____

_____

_____

_____

_____

Practice

To unlock your purpose, use the following steps to come up with your purpose sentence:

1. **LinkedIn You:** Identify and list your labels, both personal and professional.

2. **Legacy You:** How do you want to be remembered? Craft a meaningful eulogy for yourself.

3. **My Superpower:** Define your superpower (i.e., your unique gift), which is that ability or talent you excel at and do with ease.

4. **My Purpose Sentence:** Reflect on steps 1 through 3. Write a simple sentence that articulates your purpose. Feel free to use this formula:

   My purpose is [insert words from Legacy You/ My Superpower] to help [insert who or what].

Note: Once you have your purpose sentence, archive it somewhere that you will see it often to make sure you stay aligned with it.

Example

1. **LinkedIn You:**
   * Husband and dad
   * Lifelong learner
   * Student and teacher
   * Business owner
   * Avid skier
   * Lawyer

2   **Legacy You:** He lived a life that mattered. He loved his family through the good and hard times. He sought wisdom through a dedication to lifelong learning. He brought people together so they could build better communities to discover more possibility for all.

3   **My Superpower:** Connecting ideas and people.

4   **My Purpose Sentence:** My purpose is to share the wisdom of others to help people discover more possibility.

    I will put my purpose sentence as the first appointment on my schedule each day as a reminder to stay aligned with it.

7

LAUNCH
YOUR
MINDSET

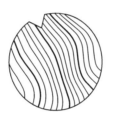

The curious explorer's mindset is the most powerful tool any of us has in the unknown, because our mindset determines the story we tell ourselves about the events we face.

SHACKLETON'S GRANDDAUGHTER once asked him about the most important qualities of an explorer.

"First optimism, secondly patience, third imagination, and fourthly, courage," he replied.

When, after being trapped in pack ice for nearly a year, their ship finally sank, Shackleton famously told his crew it was time to go home. That became their "story" for the rest of the expedition, even though at that moment they were floating on a sheet of ice out to sea. The energy of Shackleton's optimism and the grace he created with his patience, his inspiration, and his courage all enabled him to quash anxiety, motivate his crew, and get them home alive.

Our mindset is composed of the stories we tell ourselves to construct a personal sense of reality, which in turn creates the lens through which we see the world.

Some make it through the gauntlet of civilization without losing their curiosity and imagination. These are the artists, non-conformists, entrepreneurs, and creatives who see possibilities beyond the boundary that is accepted. They are constantly pushing boundaries, even when everyone says they are nuts. Their actions are motivated by curiosity and their heart's purpose, not a deductive calculus. They seek what is essential, not what is expected of them. They experiment and carry out actions just to see what will happen. The question that epitomizes their logic is, **"What if?"**

These explorer and entrepreneur qualities are components of what we call the "curious explorer's mindset." The curious explorer's mindset is the most powerful tool any of us has in the unknown, because our mindset determines the story we tell ourselves about the events we face.

Where Do We Acquire Our Mindsets in the First Place?

In school, we learn conformity. We sit in rows and stand in lines. We receive knowledge, learn how to answer the same questions in the same way, and take tests to prove it. At home, we get prompted to do the same thing, because our parents are proud of us if we follow the rules. We're taught not to screw up because, if we do, what will everyone think?

Did you win the race?

Did you get an "A" on the test?

And then it's, "What do you want to be when you grow up?" This is another way of saying, "What label can we pin on you? What will be your specialized function in the organization of your choice?"

We learn to approach challenges cognitively using deductive reasoning—a predictive style of thought. If you know the axioms and the rules, you can find every answer. You don't question the system; you live the system.

Don't rock the boat, for if you manage your tasks well and do what you're told to do, you may rise up the hierarchy. You hold off on trying new things because you need proof that it works first.

This is a mindset commonly found in our society. It's easy to resist change if you mistakenly believe the answers are already decided for you. But worry not! Despite how effective our educational and managerial designs have been in training us into standardized thinking, there is an exploratory leader lurking within every one of us.

The difference comes down to who is willing to reactivate that atrophied part of themselves and build back that muscle.

Exploratory Principle 2: Launch with a Curious Explorer's Mindset

Mindset defines the stories we tell ourselves to construct a personal sense of reality, and it is controlled by you. The mindset of a curious explorer helps us to develop stories that change outcomes for the better in the Realm of the Unknown.

At work, both managerial and exploratory mindsets are often required in order to get things done and prepare for a changing future. Exploratory leaders switch back and forth at will to adopt the mindset appropriate to the occasion. Such leaders must be mentally ambidextrous and possess dual literacy.

Read that again: Successful leaders are *dually literate*. Such leaders know how to think and act in both the known and the unknown.

How can a wannabe exploratory leader make the big transformation to adopt a curious explorer's mindset?

The good news is that it's not exactly brain surgery. Speaking of which, one of the biggest things to come out of neuroscience in the last decade is the story of the amazing neuroplasticity within the brain. It used to be that when we lost brain function due to a stroke, that was it. We couldn't talk or walk like we used to. But now we understand that neural pathways can be reformed by going around the damaged areas.

A curious explorer's mindset allows you to see more possibility.

Is adopting an explorer's mindset a matter of learning new skills? Yes and no. There are certainly basic skills to learn through practice and repetition, like storytelling. But much of this is not learning something new; it is revisiting something old in all of us. We need to unlearn some of our conformity and our bias toward prediction and bring ourselves back to our toddler brains, when we were curious and explored our way forward.

One tried-and-true way is to simply change our storyline.

Hero Teacher Michael Bungay Stanier, a man with scars, provides a compelling example of how a story can change a mindset and how a new mindset can transform a life.

I'm Scarred

BY MICHAEL BUNGAY STANIER

Your scars can hold you back and limit you. But there's another way to see them.

A scar is a story waiting to be told.

In fact, two stories.

One story of love. And its flip side, one of fear.

One of nourishment. One of diminishment.

Which story you choose to tell matters a great deal.

Let me show you what I mean. Here are two stories I tell myself about my cleft lip and palate. They're both equally true.

THE STORY OF FEAR

My cleft lip and palate means I have a speech impediment, an oddly shaped top lip, and a somewhat flattened nose.

People find me disconcerting to look at—some people see me as ugly.

People don't want to talk to me because they're uncomfortable about my cleft lip. Kids especially.

I should operate "behind the scenes" because my speech impediment means I shouldn't be "out front."

If I don't talk too much, people won't notice I have a disability. Stay quiet.

This is my disability.

THE STORY OF LOVE

My cleft lip and palate means I have a speech impediment, an oddly shaped top lip, and a somewhat flattened nose.

I stand out from the crowd. I'm not bland.

People don't notice my speech impediment. They just accept me for who I am, especially when I do what I'm best at.

When I give speeches, my unique style of speaking helps me stand out from the crowd.

People find it easier to connect to me because I have an obvious vulnerability. It balances me out, and for some people, I can be a role model for overcoming "disabilities."

This is one source of my power.

Same scars. Same person. Very different stories.

We all have scars, and each scar has different possible stories. What stories are you going to tell yourself about those scars? Those stories shape the outcome of your life.

It would have been easy for Bungay Stanier to stay in the known, grounded in the prediction that his scar would have kept him backstage. Thankfully, he explored a new possibility and told himself a story of a world where his scar would make him unique and memorable. (His complete story can be found in the book *End Malaria*.) He is gifted and successful, traveling around the globe and inspiring audiences with his amazing coaching, speeches, and bestselling books.

This is the narrative power of mindset.

At Studio/E, we use the Mindset Formula: $E + S = O$. This formula was derived from an ancient concept developed about 2,500 years ago in the philosophical school of Stoicism and has generated a deep pool of commentary over the years. "E" represents **events**. We can't change the reality of events that have occurred. "S" refers to the **stories** we tell ourselves and others about those events.

"O" is the **outcomes**. You can control the stories you tell yourself; that, in turn, changes the outcomes in front of you. Spelled out, the Mindset Formula is Events + Stories = Outcomes.

ADVISORY: CAUTION!

Adverse effects may result when the wrong mindset is applied to a situation. The application of a known mindset (the mindset of a manager) to an unknown phenomenon, such as change, may lead to irrelevance, ineffectiveness, bankruptcy, or worse. Conversely, applying an unknown mindset (the mindset of an explorer) to a known situation may cause undue irritation, commonly referred to as reinventing the wheel, fixing what isn't broken, or putting lipstick on a pig.

Often we are not intentional about the stories we tell ourselves, especially when facing the unknown, so default stories arise that are connected to fear and past failures. This happens naturally because our brain's survival mechanism wants to protect us from the unknown.

When in the unknown, intentionally framing your stories through the lens of a curious explorer is an effective way of changing outcomes so you have more possibilities to live into. This principle generates energy, excitement, and the motivation to discover more possibilities.

Mindset is the most powerful tool you possess, so use it with intention to motivate you.

LAUNCH WITH A CURIOUS EXPLORER'S MINDSET

Lesson

Mindset develops stories that change outcomes. Remember, Events + Stories (you tell yourself) = Outcomes. When in the unknown, intentionally framing your stories through the lens of a curious explorer is an effective way of changing outcomes so you have more possibilities to live into. A curious explorer's mindset produces motivation.

Question

What mindset stories are you telling yourself?

_____

_____

_____

_____

_____

_____

_____

Practice

To craft your curious-explorer's-mindset story when in the unknown, use the following steps:

1. **Curious-Explorer's-Mindset Words:** Think of three words that might represent your own curious explorer's mindset. What words generate energy, excitement, and motivation for you? Write these words down.

2. **Negative Story:** What's a story you tell yourself that has a *negative* effect on you?

3. **Curious-Explorer's-Mindset Story:** Tell that same story as a curious explorer with your three curious-explorer's-mindset words so that it has a *positive* effect on you.

Example

1. **Curious-Explorer's-Mindset Words:** Curiosity, generosity, growth

2. **Negative Story:** When I launch new ideas that I don't know how to fully build at the beginning, it is nerve-racking and intimidating. People will probably think I am not prepared. They might think I am faking it or maybe I'm not talented enough to do this.

3. **Curious-Explorer's-Mindset Story:** Launching new ideas helps me and others grow and discover what is possible. My curiosity and generosity are huge assets for discovering how I can help others think differently and launch new ideas. If I'm up front with others about the reason for exploring an idea rather than trying to perfectly plan it, people will be accepting and engaged with the process.

8

BUILD AN
EXPLORATORY
LEARNING
COMMUNITY

If you want to navigate more effectively, **hang out with people who know things you don't.**

FROM HIS prior expeditions, Shackleton had learned the ineffectiveness of hierarchy and a homogeneous crew when plans go awry. A rigid structure and a lack of diversity don't allow for agility. And agility is what we need to generate innovation in every aspect of work and life.

In fact, Shackleton reviewed thousands of candidates for the crew and selected people with different skills, experiences, and relationships. Only five of the twenty-eight crew members on the *Endurance* were able seamen. The crew actually included individuals who had no previous sailing experience, such as an artist, a doctor, a scientist, a carpenter, a mechanic, and a meteorologist who played the banjo.

The diversity of talents and experiences on board, coupled with the dually literate genius of Shackleton, allowed the crew to pivot into new approaches frequently during their ordeal. This diversity allowed the crew to look at their challenges from different perspectives. In part, it's what enabled them all to live, surmounting the heavy odds against them.

In the Realm of the Unknown, effective teams are intentionally assembled with diverse talent who have different experiences and know-how.

If you want to navigate more effectively, hang out with people who know things you don't. A common characteristic of leaders who excel in navigating ambiguity is a commitment to ongoing learning with diverse lenses. Effective leaders intentionally create or join multidimensional learning teams or communities and they are actively engaged within them. Hybridity of experiences, skills, and relationships always allows us to compare, contrast, include, and learn. A culture of trust takes hold within these communities and gives rise to inspiration, resilience, and growth.

It may be quite comfortable sticking with people like yourself, but it is also the antithesis of the curious explorer's mindset. Explorers constantly thrust themselves into the unknown, and often it can be quite uncomfortable. Exploring is an exciting adventure, and slight discomfort gives way to exhilaration and manifold possibilities.

For example, when NASA wants to find the exact location of a spacecraft, one radio telescope is not enough. They need two. They send signals to the spacecraft from widely separated parts of the planet (say, California and Spain), and then they correlate those measurements with a constant object, such as a pulsar. This process is called triangulation—and it works for humans too.

You may have a certain perspective on an issue and a certain amount of knowledge about it, but what if you sought out the perspective of another? That's knowledge squared. And a third person? You might even be talking about knowledge to the tenth power, given how many different ideas you might come up with as a team. You can power up your knowledge by communicating with other people who have distinctly different perspectives and world views. After all, NASA doesn't put two radio telescopes next to each other in California. That would be redundant, not to mention useless.

Exploratory Principle 3: Launch with an Exploratory Learning Community

Being a member of an exploratory learning community expands possibility.

An exploratory learning community is an aligned group of people who each have a diverse set of experiences and knowledge. Their skills and understanding grow by regularly meeting and engaging in reciprocal conversation and mutual guidance. They are driven by high expectations, professionalism, and peer accountability that generate transformative value within the organization and with those affected by their work.

If the task of the explorer is to venture successfully into the unknown, we'd better be very clear on what we know and what we don't know.

Another Hero Teacher, Erik Gabrielson, leads a great organization focused on creating resilient and thriving teams, called Activ8. He reminded us that knowledge can be divided into three main territories:

1   That which you know you know (a known)

2   That which you know you don't know (a known unknown)

3   That which you don't even know you don't know (an unknown unknown)

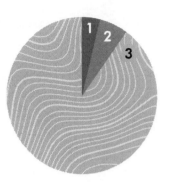

For example, when you set off on an expedition, you have a basic knowledge of the terrain and the climate, but you may not be sure how many days it will take you. That length is a known unknown. You can prepare for that by bringing extra provisions. But you may encounter an unforeseen obstacle such as a ravenous wolf pack. That would be an unknown unknown. But perhaps someone in your multidimensional learning community has been on a similar expedition and can give you a heads-up on the possibility of wolves and how to successfully survive an encounter with them.

An exploratory learning community is a network that is critical to expanding your knowledge and experience so you can navigate the unknown. Our networks, and how active we decide to be within them, are a primary predictor of leadership success. During our life's pursuits, when we include others with diverse experiences, skills, and relationships, we expand our access to knowledge. That, in turn, provides more wisdom to draw upon for any trek into the unknown, enhancing our chances for success.

Building trust means letting people get beyond their titles and share their humanity. A lack of trust slows progress and wastes resources. Jimmy Chin explains that, in mountaineering, he always has trust on the agenda, but he also trusts in the process.

"A lot of the trust that we need on the mountain is developed over time," he explains. "So, often the case is that if you are climbing with a new partner, you start on smaller climbs. Climbing can be used as a metaphor for everything we do. On climbs, you can see how your interactions go, you can see what kind of decisions people make together. And a big part of trust is understanding where everybody's risk threshold lies. So you understand their decision making, but sometimes trust can happen very quickly."

And on a mountain, just like in life, a lot of trust can be measured through unspoken acts.

"If you watch someone tie a knot, you watch them build an anchor, you watch how they belay, you look at what kind of gear they chose for the rack, you know that you can trust someone pretty quickly," Chin told us. "It goes without saying you have to have a lot of trust to even start a climb, because you're trusting that someone new is going to be able to get you off the mountain if something happens and vice versa. But in knowing myself, I trust that I'm surrounded by a peer group of people who are very experienced, and I know that the baseline is very, very high."

The wisest people on our planet trust themselves because they know how little they know. Our ignorance of the unknown is a great source of humility, but it is also a bottomless source of possibilities. We can greatly amplify our knowledge by sharing our perspectives with different people and trusting that we're going to keep learning. If you want to learn, grow, and expand your possibilities, jumpstart your curiosity and motivation by interacting with people from many walks of life.

LAUNCH WITH AN EXPLORATORY LEARNING COMMUNITY

Lesson

An exploratory learning community expands possibility. Remember, if you want to expand your knowledge, hang out with people who know things you don't. An exploratory learning community produces motivation and ongoing support for its members.

Question

Which exploratory learning community supports you?

_____

_____

_____

_____

_____

_____

_____

Practice

To create and facilitate your own exploratory learning community, follow the steps below:

1   **Recruitment:** Recruit and enroll two or three smart, diversely experienced people who commit to meet monthly to inspire, advise, tackle challenges, and solve problems together and follow the Exploratory Learning Community Framework.

2   **Exploratory Learning Community Framework:** Use this framework to guide your exploratory learning community:

   * **Schedule your monthly meeting.** Set up a monthly virtual or in-person sixty-minute meeting. For each meeting, the group designates a meeting leader. The assigned leader sends out a calendar invite to the group, runs the agenda, and takes notes.

   * **Share inspiration.** To kick off the meeting, the leader shares something inspirational, like a quote, thought, or experience they have had and why it's a favorite.

   * **Do a two-minute check-in.** Each member shares something positive (a "rose") and a challenge (a "thorn") that has happened since the last meeting.

   * **Review priorities.** Each member shares one of their most important priorities (personal or professional) over the last thirty days and what obstacles they are facing. The other members provide helpful

feedback and advice on what they could do to get around their obstacles.

- **Make final declarations.** Each member declares up to three priorities (personal or professional) they would like to work on between now and the next meeting. The leader archives the declarations and sends them out via email after the meeting. Note: The priorities should be clear and concise and include a date of desired completion.

- **Schedule your next meeting.** The group schedules the upcoming month's meeting and assigns a new leader.

Example

1   **Recruitment:** I will recruit and enroll Kevin (teacher), Rip (writer), and Lani (leadership development expert) to form an exploratory learning community, and we will help each other navigate our challenges and celebrate our successes. These awesome souls are very different from me, yet I have deep respect for each of them, and we are all aligned in our commitment to lifelong learning.

2   **Exploratory Learning Community Framework:** Our new group will meet on a regular monthly cadence, and we will use the Exploratory Learning Community Framework to facilitate our meetings.

9

NAVIGATE

YOUR

PACKAGED

IDEA MVPS

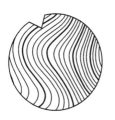

Exploratory leaders take one small step into the unknown at a time, which provides enough clarity to plan the subsequent steps needed to clearly explore, launch, and navigate.

WHEN DISASTER struck the expedition, Shackleton broke down the challenge into small steps, because big steps required dangerous assumptions.

Shackleton and his crew regularly measured the food stores, equipment, weather patterns, their progress, their coordinates, and many other things, so they always knew where they stood. This clarity produced a sense of safety. This became critical since on many days during their ordeal they would actually lose ground because the rotating ice under their feet would turn in the wrong direction. Keeping track of their whereabouts and their resources allowed them to constantly explore new ways to survive, take small actions, and navigate through challenges until they found their way home.

Shackleton's mission as an exploratory leader was to cut loose from known-world thinking, tools, and principles in order to launch an idea expedition into the unknown.

To emulate Shackleton, we have to understand the concept of MVP, or minimum viable progress. The minimum viable progress concept is from the must-read book *Essentialism*, by Greg McKeown.

An idea in its initial stages in the unknown is quite vague. It can include any type of concept, opinion, belief, challenge, or invention. That's why, in the known world, we also need to have something to grab on to. What is the smallest amount of progress that will be useful for you to learn more about an idea over a selected period of time? Think baby steps, experiments, tests, and small prototypes for the elements of an idea expedition into the unknown. That's what we're talking about.

The reason we need to check in with our MVP is that it is a given that our brains will initially react negatively to expeditions into the unknown. The brain does not like the ambiguity that lies ahead and deeply desires enough clarity to calmly look at what's to come. Exploratory leaders do this by taking one small step into the unknown at a time. This provides enough clarity to plan the subsequent steps needed to clearly *explore*, *launch*, and *navigate*. This is a concept from the excellent book *The Lean Startup*, by Eric Ries. He talks about MVP as minimum viable *product*. McKeown takes that concept and applies it more broadly to minimum viable progress. When coming up with an idea, we need to think of it in terms of small bits of *progress*.

Exploratory Principle 4:
Navigate with Packaged Idea MVPs

An idea expedition is an idea you want to explore, launch, and navigate. There are three elements to packaging your idea expeditions into the Realm of the Unknown. Those elements are an idea name, idea MVP, and metrics, and together they create a Packaged Idea MVP.

Name your idea. As we face the changing needs of humans and their challenges and crises in this rapidly changing world, we will have many innovative ideas to explore, launch, and navigate. The first element to packaging your idea expedition is to name your idea, something you want to explore next. Give it an identity and a personality so that it becomes mobile, clear, and easy for others to grasp and share effectively. The biggest mistake we see when people launch ideas is they wait too long to name them. Name your idea something punchy, unique, and memorable. Temporary names are good. The marketing department can always change the name later.

Identify your idea MVP. Ask yourself: What is the smallest amount of progress that will be useful and valuable to move my idea expedition forward? The strategy is to take a small step, not a perfect step. Great exploratory leaders think in terms of better, not perfect. Remember, we're looking for momentum at this point; perfection will only slow us down.

To do this, you'll need to dissect your idea into small steps. Identify an MVP for one of those steps. Think about what you must learn in order to move your idea forward over a small period of time (such as thirty days). Then you will gain valuable learnings by conducting an MVP.

Some examples of idea MVPs:

* Conducting a beta experiment
* Running an A/B test
* Sending out a client survey or interviews
* Assessing your data outside of an automatic process
* Creating one-page brochures to get feedback
* Trying out a new call-to-action pitch
* Developing an endcap to test a product in a store
* Running a learning salon
* Mind mapping
* Constructing a storyboard or run of show

What you are trying to accomplish with an idea MVP is a small step that produces clarity of what to do next over a specific period of time.

It's quite likely that at first it may strike you as too simplistic or slow to move with a single step. Don't worry. You won't be making just one simple, single step. More likely than not, your idea expedition will require conducting several idea MVPs (in other words, multiple steps) in parallel, in sequence, or both. We typically use thirty days for an idea MVP step, but the time frame can be anything that allows you to complete the idea MVP. Some idea MVPs can be achieved in five days, and others might take longer than a month. It all depends on the idea MVP. During a tight deadline or crisis, idea MVP time frames can be daily or hourly. All of these steps may be related, but by pulling them apart into specific, viable, and minimum goals, you can create much more clarity that will lead to progressive momentum. One of the greatest human motivators is to make progress, and if you break ideas into small steps (idea MVPs), you will consistently make progress.

Track your progress with metrics. Metrics create a scoreboard, a count of how many experiments are undertaken, or an archiving of the lessons learned over a period of time for your idea MVP. Think about what you actually want to be accountable to, and your creative mind will allow you to come up with many ways to show how you are producing value out of your idea expeditions. Conducting measurements surrounding our explorations helps us navigate and stay on course. Metrics allow us to track our progress in a clear and objective way. This makes us accountable on our idea expeditions so we can meet our expectations with each idea MVP and achieve the results we desire.

When exploratory leaders drop the need to see the whole solution to their idea at the beginning, they can proceed under the radar, as it were, to build their design gradually over a series of iterations—each of them a small step. It can be hard for smart people with big ideas to think small, but doing so creates momentum. Allow the design to emerge over time. Rapid small steps almost always beat the big leap when we're exploring in the

Realm of the Unknown. It is also easier to get started. Remember, "explore" is a verb, so you're not really an explorer until you actually start exploring.

Ideas become bigger when moved through small steps.

ADVISORY: CAUTION!

Typical Realm of the Known metrics are return on investment (ROI), quality measures, efficiency measures, et cetera. They are extremely valuable and necessary. As a general exploratory rule, lagging metrics, which measure past performance, are often better for the Realm of the Known, whereas leading metrics, which set benchmarks to be met, are often better for the Realm of the Unknown. The Achilles' heel of Realm of the Known metrics is they can drive behavior that is not always wanted. Beware! Sometimes metrics are confused with strategy. Even worse, they can unknowingly become an organization's strategy. Metrics are not strategy; they measure the outcome of an organization's strategy.

Metrics in the Unknown

Even in the unknown, you can create effective metrics.

Explorer Tyler Fish, another Hero Teacher, told us that he created a novel metric to help him and his partner John Huston reach the North Pole by their deadline.

Time was running out on their bid to be the first Americans to reach the North Pole unassisted. The skiers knew they could ski for half of every day, but given the distance to their goal and the changes they faced with the rotating ice, there weren't enough days left. Their solution was to invent a radically new metric that redefined the definition of a day. Instead of twenty-four hours, a day would be thirty hours. That increased their half-day skiing session from twelve hours to fifteen hours. This new metric worked! It allowed them to reach the Pole in time.

Realm of the Unknown metrics heighten our awareness of what we are actually doing and can convey something tangible to our stakeholders. Think of Realm of the Unknown metrics as a measure of accountability.

The metrics of the Realm of the Unknown are quite unlike metrics in the Realm of the Known, but to have metrics at all heightens one's credibility immensely in the eye of the stakeholder. Metrics in the Realm of the Known are almost exclusively about quantifiable facts presented with numbers. This accords with the emphasis on certainty, for nothing is more certain than mathematics. Two plus two is surely going to add up to four wherever you go.

But metrics don't always have to be numbers, especially in the Realm of the Unknown; they can be personal standards of behavior, boundaries, or guiding principles. Oftentimes, they are merely the act of tracking our inputs and what we learned along the way. Realm of the Unknown metrics are the mile markers of progress in the unknown.

Some examples of metrics for the Realm of the Unknown include the following.

MVP metrics (make these specific to the applicable MVP):

* Feedback from a certain number of participants on idea beta experiments

* Select the top three key findings and the needs from A/B tests

* Identify a certain number of needed elements on the idea's current design

* Share a call-to-action pitch with several stakeholders for insights

Exploration metrics (make these applicable to all your exploration activities):

* Tuition (the amount of money you are willing to invest to learn)

* The number and type of new networks formed (inside and outside your organization)

* The number of ideas you've launched, killed, and pivots you've made

* Identify behaviors that create incentive to explore

Exploratory leaders always have metrics to track their performance and accountability for both realms. You cannot manage or direct what you don't measure, no matter what realm you are in.

NAVIGATE WITH
PACKAGED IDEA MVPS

Lesson

Packaged idea MVPs—focusing on small steps over short periods of time—create clarity, valuable learning, and effective progress through the unknown. Small actions can lead to really big things.

Question

What is your packaged idea MVP?

_____

_____

_____

_____

_____

_____

_____

Practice

Identify an idea you would like to explore or launch but that you're not quite sure how to move forward. Then, package that idea following these steps:

1 **Idea Name:** Name your idea.

2 **Idea MVP:** Identify an idea MVP step (and time frame) that will move your idea forward.

3 **MVP Metric(s):** Establish what you will measure to ensure you are making progress on your idea MVP.

Example

I want to create a leadership program that helps leaders courageously explore the unknown.

1 **Idea Name:** Expedition Program

2 **Idea MVP:** Create a run of show for beta day of the Expedition Program over the next thirty days. (A "run of show" is a production schedule for an event that identifies the content to be presented, the presenter, and the time frames for the presentation. A "beta day" is a test day used to learn what would work within an official program launch day.)

3 **MVP Metric:** Identify at least seven content modules in the run of show.

10

ASK

EXPLORATORY
QUESTIONS

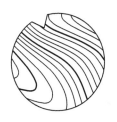

If you're going to be
a great exploratory leader,
**keep curiosity on the
front burner and stow
those judgments in
the ice box.**

SHACKLETON'S EXPEDITION could use only what it had on hand.

Shackleton made sure each crew member had a specific role and responsibility that used their unique skills and talents. Yet even those roles were subject to change depending on the situation, which was, shall we say, *fluid*. All crew members contributed something at all times.

As there were no instructions on how to get back home, Shackleton and his crew began experimenting with new ideas using their existing materials. For example, they built a base camp on ice, invented new ways to cook, turned a lifeboat into a sailboat, and turned other lifeboats into shelter. They also knew they were part of a heroic story, captured by the team's photographer and their own diaries.

By all accounts, Shackleton was admired by most of his crew. He enjoyed a reputation as an experienced explorer who took care of everyone. He simply refused to sacrifice a crew member in order to achieve the expedition's goals (even though doing so was common practice in those days!). His outspoken insistence on life over death endeared him to the crew and was an important way of creating safety and trust for them all. And, given the situation they were in, there was always someone who took on a task at a moment's notice regardless of the challenge. During the many months of the expedition, Shackleton repeatedly enrolled his crew in new activities that contributed to learning their way home.

What we learn from this iterative process is that the art of exploration is a perpetual quest, along with a perpetual set of exploratory questions. Exploratory questions focus the action you will take to move through the unknown, and Shackleton and his leaders constantly asked exploratory questions, questions that created more possibility.

Great questions can prompt amazing insights and break down entrenched thinking. And one of the primary reasons to ask a question is to bring awareness to what we don't know.

Exploratory Principle 5:
Navigate with Exploratory Questions

As Michael Bungay Stanier once told us, "Great questions elevate the way you lead, the way you influence, and your outcomes."

Exploratory questions differ considerably from the typical questions in the known world, because our most important questions do not always have immediate, clear answers. Our ultimate question is the quest itself, not a mere interrogatory sentence; our exploratory questions can only be answered by taking an action to journey into the unknown and discovering the result when we get there. Our best questions inspire and focus clear actions, not more words.

Multiple choice questions, yes-or-no questions, or anything similar may be useful in the known world, but they just don't do the job when you're exploring in the unknown. Warren Berger, in his book *A More Beautiful Question*, defines a "beautiful question" as an ambitious yet actionable question that can begin to shift the way we perceive or think about something—a question that might serve as a catalyst to bring about change.

The mode of thought for the exploratory leader is one of questioning for discovery, and the first thing we question are the hidden presuppositions of the conventional wisdom of the known world. We know the known world's addiction to certainty is based on an illusion, because change is the only certainty. This opens our minds to a wide range of possibility, fires up our curiosity, and frees our imagination.

Questions help to clarify the direction of our focus and enable us to flesh out an idea or more possibility, which becomes the target of our quest. Exploratory leaders become curious explorers of what their stakeholders need, not what they already know how to do. They stay aligned with their purpose and create clear and safe pathways for their expedition into the unknown. They get wonderful, energetic minds to join them because such minds deeply desire to walk that path with them.

Make Sure Your Question Is Actually a Question

Have you ever heard a question that looks like this: "Are you really going to wear that?" Or perhaps you've heard this one: "What were you thinking?" You guessed it. Those aren't questions! Despite the cute punctuation marks at the end of those sentences, they are actually judgments. You can't judge and be curious at the same time. If you're going to be a great exploratory leader, keep curiosity on the front burner and stow those judgments in the ice box.

And don't ask "How?" first.

"How?" is an important but secondary question, and if you ask it too soon, it can derail your effort. The most important exploratory question is "Why?" because that locates your purpose, your ultimate aim. Your "why" may be unique. It may be an "only," but there are many ways to get there. For example, we launched the Studio/E Expedition Program based on the unique belief that we would help leaders and their teams courageously explore the unknown to discover more possibility in a rapidly changing world. This was a unique perspective on leadership development. We did not know how to do that initially.

"What if?" and "Who?" are other great questions that prompt exploration. There is always more than one "how," and you don't want to get bogged down in the pros and cons before it's time. After you explore with other, more open-ended questions, end your inquiry with a nice chaser of "How?"

But let's dig deeper. Being competent is the ability to do something successfully or efficiently. Studying the lives and experiences of entrepreneurs and explorers, we've found that four competencies always seem to be present in some form: current means, ideation, boundaries, and enrollment. We have exploratory questions based on each of these competencies that focus the actions exploratory leaders should take in the Realm of the Unknown.

Current means. *What do you have to put toward your idea right now?* What assets do you have? Specifically, what do you currently have in terms of materials, experiences, skills, and relationships to put toward your idea? This is an asset-based thinking approach that allows for a quick launch of an idea by relying only upon the resources and tools already on hand. You can avoid the lost time that would be spent waiting to acquire other tools or resources. Think widely about what constitutes an asset. Be sure to consider your experiences, relationships, and skills.

During his days as an emerging artist, multimedia artist Phil Hansen's love of pointillism was jeopardized by the thousands of repetitive hand movements it took to create those little dots. He developed a tremor that was diagnosed as permanent nerve damage. His career was disrupted, and he feared it was over. However, after some advice from a doctor, Hansen decided to "Embrace the Shake." (Be sure to watch his TED Talk of the same title.) Once he accepted his new method of making art, new waves of energy and creativity surged inside him. Hansen's current means carved out a new area for his artistic creativity, and it put his career back on track in a new, valuable direction.

Ideation. *What makes your idea of unique value to its users?* Specifically, what unique ability do you and your idea have to address the needs of its users? Ideation is the act of generating ideas. Great ideas solve someone's pain points or create new value. Famously, we are told there is no "I" in "team." Never mind, because there is an "I" in "ideation."

The best ideas are unique, differentiated, and individualized to meet the needs of their users. As Hero Teacher Ryan Holiday explains, "People get way too consumed with whatever is trendy and cool right now. And what they don't think about is: How long was that trend in development? And how long is it likely to continue to be here? Yeah. When you are creating ideas or brands that are built to last, you are the trend curve. 'Only' is better than 'best.'"

Boundaries. *What are you willing (and not willing) to invest in your idea to take the next step?* Specifically, what are you willing to do, and what are you *not* willing to do to move this idea forward? Boundaries are your declared parameters when exploring the unknown. Boundaries create pathways that provide clarity, safety, and confidence.

World-class open-water swimmer Lynne Cox established boundaries by drawing a line in the water. That was her successful strategy when she became the first person to swim across the Strait of Magellan in southern Chile. To become acclimated to the frigid temperatures, Cox put time limits on how long she would stay in the extremely cold water during her preparation. She broke the process down into a precise sequence of small steps. She swam a little longer each time. Yes, it might seem quicker just to take a Polar Bear Plunge, but as Cox says, when you leap big, you can fail big. It is much wiser to go from small step to small step until you meet your goal. Boundaries will help you establish your path forward in the Realm of the Unknown.

Enrollment. *Who can make your idea better, and why would they help?* Specifically, who can you enroll that would be interested in helping you identify and address the needs of your new idea? Enrollment is the art of inviting another to combine their purpose with yours. Enrollment is a catalyst and an accelerator. The magnetic rule for enrolling others requires empathy: Treat others how *they* want to be treated *and inspired*.

Hero Teacher Dan Roam points out that enrollment can be enhanced by expressing your ideas with visual imagery. If an entire cerebral hemisphere is devoted to visual thinking, why do we reduce ourselves to only using words to communicate our ideas? It's like tying half our brain behind our back. We have been surviving via visual thinking since the dawn of humanity. Written words are relatively new. We have found drawings dating back 40,000 years, while the first written word is only 5,000 years old, and even then, the early scripts were pictographs. You don't need a cave wall; just get yourself a white board or draw pictures in your journal. If you can make a circle, a line, a square, and a triangle, you can create a drawing to effectively enroll others in your vision. Drawing clarifies thinking, and it allows others to see what you imagine. Clarity makes others feel safe and allows them to embrace and remember your idea. See, for example, how we used these simple shapes to create symbols for each principle of Exploratory Leadership.

Drawing simple shapes   Examples of creating symbols from drawing shapes

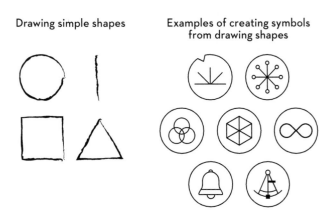

Exploratory questions create clarity that reveal more possibility to explore. The best exploratory questions are those that can only be answered by taking more action. They focus you on key areas to explore. The destination of your quest can be discovered through exploratory questions and then action. The question is the quest.

Let's do it and find out.

NAVIGATE WITH EXPLORATORY QUESTIONS

Lesson

Exploratory questions focus action. Remember, exploratory questions create clarity that reveals more possibility so you have more opportunities to explore.

Questions

What exploratory questions are you asking?

_____

_____

_____

_____

_____

_____

_____

_____

Practice

Answer these exploratory questions for your idea MVPs with the following steps:

1 **Idea MVP:** Identify your idea MVP.

2 **Exploratory Questions:** Brainstorm answers to the following exploratory questions about your idea MVP.

   * **Current means:** What do you have to put toward your idea right now? (Think about your experience, skills, and relationships.)

   * **Ideation:** What makes your idea of unique value to its users?

   * **Boundaries:** What are you willing to invest (and not invest) in your idea to take the next step?

   * **Enrollment:** Who can make your idea better, and why would they help?

Example

1 **Idea MVP:** Create a run of show for beta day of the Expedition Program.

2 **Exploratory Questions:**

   * **Current means:**

     Attended great leadership programs and coached teams.

     Have done public speaking and provided counsel for leaders.

Worked with many thought leaders, corporate leaders, teachers, and entrepreneurs.

- **Ideation:** This idea will inspire leaders and their teams to courageously explore unknown realms to discover more possibility.

- **Boundaries:**

  Time: 10 to 20 hours

  Money: $0 to $100 for lunches

  I will share run of show with two thought leaders in the leadership development space for feedback. I will not share this with potential sponsors until later.

- **Enrollment:** I will enroll two thought leaders, Cheryl and Heidi, as they have created many successful programs and are interested in exploration to help others grow.

11

DECLARE

ACTION

Action is not about getting it right at first; it's about creating momentum so you keep going to make it right.

EACH DAY ON their derailed expedition to cross Antarctica, Shackleton declared action for each member of the crew, himself included.

From the declared action, they learned what was working and what was not and built a plan for the next step. This principle created momentum, which was needed to survive. They declared action each day over and over again until something worked. Many times, the initial action failed, so they tried something else. They never stopped experimenting and improvising until they all were rescued.

But in between the time the crew got stuck and the time they were rescued, a lot of action had to take place as things got more desperate. The *Endurance* couldn't withstand the breaking apart of the spring ice. The crew had stayed steadfast for ten months waiting to free their ship, but when the hull began to disintegrate on October 27, 1915, they found themselves camping on the ice floe for another five months. What had been a salvage mission quickly became mired in the fear that accompanies a new, unknown challenge, because the ice floe melted as it headed out to sea.

When they couldn't stay any longer on the ice floe, Shackleton's twenty-eight-person crew launched three lifeboats, which they finally landed hundreds of miles away at Elephant Island. On their row to freedom, a non-stop endeavor of many days, Shackleton handed over his mittens to photographer Frank Hurley. Shackleton left himself to suffer frostbite so that Hurley would not lose his ability to keep documenting their adventure, yet another example of Shackleton's purpose in action.

It was there, on the tiny, remote, and inhospitable Elephant Island, with a fraction of their original supplies, that Shackleton declared action on a seemingly wild idea to lead his crew to a final push in order to save their lives.

Nothing happens without action. Period.

Coming up with a good idea isn't all that hard. Putting an idea into action is where things get real. Action is messy, and in the unknown, it takes courage.

Exploratory Principle 6: Navigate with Declared Action

Action is doing something to achieve an aim. Unfortunately, many of us don't aim.

The core of success in navigating the unknown is something we call "declared action." A declaration is a statement that starts with "We will…" or "I will…" The declaration defines a future state.

Action is not about getting it right at first; it's about creating momentum so you keep going to make it right. Declared action generates momentum. When we have momentum, we create confidence. Think about those small action steps toward a bigger idea (our idea MVPs). Action creates new pathways of possibility so that we can learn where to go next and where not to go next. Action focuses our mind on the present so that we have real things to observe and don't waste our time mulling over assumptions that accompany non-action.

In this way, words are more than tools that name and describe things; they can change your future. The way to do that is to craft your words into effective declarations that can be converted into accountable and focused actions. Actions bring declarations into reality. That is why we call this principle "declared action."

Quite simply, what actions will you declare to move your idea forward?

Things don't have to be complex to be valuable. For example, imagine if your idea expedition is to create a new leadership program and your idea MVP is to design a run of show for a beta day of that program. Your current means include attending other leadership programs and using a run-of-show format and timeline from a different event as resources. Your declared action for those current means could be this: "I [noun] will design [verb] a run of show for beta day based on the format I have within the next four days [date]." Although this example seems basic, many influential leaders get stuck on what to do initially when in the unknown and create complex plans, rather than taking action to learn what is next.

In the same way, beware of the misguided defense mechanism of waiting for complete certainty as you "get ready." Many people just keep getting ready and never take action. Although we all want certainty, that is not available in the Realm of the Unknown—but we can create clarity. Action precedes clarity in the unknown. Taking declared action is the key to generating the momentum to discover more possibility.

"Aim High, Take Action, and Ignore the Noise"

Dr. Harold Brown, teacher, Tuskegee airman, and one of our most respected Hero Teachers, was shot down over enemy territory while serving in World War II as part of the 332nd Fighter Group.

To understand his story and the actions he took, we have to go back a bit further. Because of the fact that our military was segregated at the time, what Dr. Brown experienced in a prisoner-of-war camp was unique.

So what's Dr. Brown's backstory?

Booker T. Washington, a freed slave from Virginia, attended the Hampton Normal and Agricultural Institute. There, he was exposed to one of the best examples of vocational education in the nation. At that time, Hampton focused its efforts on preparing young Black men throughout the South to fill jobs in the skilled trades. Washington became an apprentice of Hampton's president and decided to lead his own school after graduating. In 1881, he took the helm at the fledgling Tuskegee Institute, where Dr. Brown eventually trained to be one of the first Black military pilots in the United States, as well as an electronics officer. He was drawn to the school because Tuskegee had quickly become famous for its practical curriculum in the mechanical trades. As a proponent of Black advancement through vocational training and racial reconciliation, Washington believed firmly that the best way for formerly enslaved people to attain equality in the United States was through the accumulation of power, wealth, and respect by means of hard work.

Almost thirty years after Booker T. Washington's death, Dr. Brown found himself in that POW camp with men from the United States, Canada, Australia, England, and many other Allied corps. And it was the first time during his military career that Dr. Brown lived, ate, and shared stories with white men facing the same challenges he was facing. They were in the fight together.

"I find it more than a little ironic that it took someone going into a prisoner-of-war camp to have your first taste of desegregation," Dr. Brown told us. "But you know, it was those men who came back from that experience of living a desegregated experience that kicked off the civil rights movement. So they didn't just fight a war abroad, they actually brought peace back here and started a really good war here."

Action creates momentum that stimulates the energy needed to fight challenges amid a crisis, or, similarly, to launch new ideas that are resisted by others. In understanding what was possible when they had nothing left to lose under the control of an enemy, Dr. Brown and others recognized the possibility in front of them to declare action.

"So the prejudice and all the other things that was going on? How did I deal with that? And didn't that get in the way? Nothing got in the way," Dr. Brown explained.

"When I came back from the front, I had my own goals, or objectives. And the only way I knew I was going to get through was that every ounce of energy I had was going to be concentrated on that goal."

Dr. Brown's civil rights legacy is still standing. Our home city of Minneapolis was ground zero for an international crisis in the wake of the murder of George Floyd in 2020. Millions of people around the globe took to the streets spontaneously. What did they call for? Declared action.

In fact, the chief diversity officer of a large bank in Minneapolis, Greg Cunningham, another one of our Hero Teachers carrying on Dr. Brown's legacy, responded to that call with three declared actions to address racial inequity that would start right away. But it wasn't easy for him, just like it wasn't easy for Dr. Brown.

"I processed first from a cultural perspective, being Black and male in America," Cunningham admitted. "I was terrified."

He demanded three things:

* Commit to hiring minority talent within organizations.

* Denounce systemic racism.

* Support minority small businesses and close the wealth gap in our society.

These three actions are clear and generate momentum for both Cunningham and those he influences.

"We are sitting on a moment in history when this notion of inclusion is the biggest business opportunity that's ever been in front of us," Cunningham said.

As we say, changing our activities generates a change in the way we think. It's a lot easier and a lot quicker to act your way into new thinking than to try to think yourself into a new way of acting.

Your declarations prompt the kind of actions that move your idea forward and create confidence. Declared action reframes your obstacles, opening new pathways to possibility. If we could give just one piece of advice to every young person in the world, it would be this: Live a life of declared action fueled by your purpose.

Rather than waiting to understand everything and plan for the perfect time to launch, it's better to get into immediate action. With action, your exploration is in motion.

NAVIGATE WITH DECLARED ACTION

Lesson

Action precedes clarity in the unknown. Declaring action generates momentum, which in turn creates confidence.

Question

What is the declared action for your idea MVP?

_____

_____

_____

_____

_____

_____

_____

_____

Practice

To declare action for your idea MVP, follow these steps:

1   **Idea MVP:** Identify your idea MVP.

2   **Declared Action:** Given the four exploratory competencies (current means, ideation, boundaries, and enrollment—see Exploratory Principle 5), craft a declared action for your idea MVP that includes a noun, verb, and date.

Example

1   **Idea MVP:** Create a run of show for beta day of the Expedition Program.

2   **Declared Action:**

   * **Current means:** I will design a run of show (draft 1) for beta day loosely based on (not copying) the formats I have from other leadership programs within the next four days.

   * **Ideation:** I will include a story of a courageous explorer within the content of the run of show within the next seven days.

   * **Boundaries:** I will finalize the run of show so that it can be shared for feedback with thought leaders in the next fourteen days.

   * **Enrollment:** I will share the run of show with two thought leaders, Cheryl and Heidi, and incorporate their overall feedback, and I will have at least seven content modules within the next thirty days.

12

POWER

YOUR

REFLECTION

Reflection creates compound learning, which in turn generates deep confidence.

REGARDLESS OF whether the day was successful or not, Shackleton used his diary to reflect most days and consider the next step on the journey.

Shackleton's and his crew's diaries are a revealing read of what they were experiencing and how Shackleton decided to show up as a leader. Every day produced important new information that could be constantly applied going forward.

When the crew reached Elephant Island, Shackleton declared action to create a sailboat from one of the lifeboats and sail it to an inhabited whaling station on South Georgia Island 780 miles away—a brand-new idea MVP. The crew quickly fixed and equipped one of the three lifeboats with sails, and taking five of the crew with him, Shackleton packed supplies for only weeks. Shackleton gave himself that boundary because if they didn't meet that goal, there was no coming back in time to achieve their goal of saving the rest of the crew, who had very few supplies themselves. On April 24, 1916 (462 days since their ship was caught in the ice), the small team set off for South Georgia, soon to be facing hurricane-force winds that damned a 500-ton steamer, a ship a thousand times their boat's size, on a parallel voyage.

Map of Shackleton's Imperial Trans-Antarctic Expedition

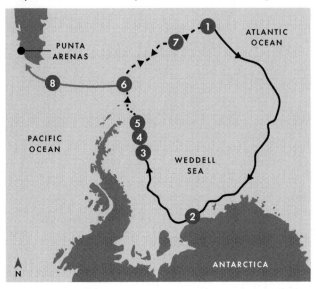

—— *Endurance* route

••••• Route of lifeboats

— — — Route of *James Caird* lifeboat

▬▬▬ Rescue to Chile

1. Expedition begins from South Georgia Island, Dec. 5, 1914.

2. *Endurance* trapped in ice, Jan. 18, 1915. Drifting for almost 10 months.

3. *Endurance* crushed; crew abandons ship, Oct. 27, 1915. Camped on melting ice for 5 months.

4. *Endurance* sinks, Nov. 21, 1915.

5. Crew launches 3 lifeboats from the melting ice camp for Elephant Island, Apr. 9, 1916. Arrive 6 days later.

6. Shackleton and 5 crew sail *James Caird* lifeboat to South Georgia, Apr. 24, 1916.

7. The 6 crew reach South Georgia Island May 10, 1916, and 3 of the men traverse mountain to whaling station.

8. Remainder of the crew rescued from Elephant Island, Aug. 30, 1916.

Unbelievably, after two weeks of sailing in the most violent sea in the world, the small crew made it to South Georgia Island, the island they had initially departed from seventeen and a half months earlier. Unfortunately, they landed on the wrong side of the mostly uninhabited island, and a mountain stood between them and the whaling station they aimed to reach to secure their safety. Leaving half the team at their landing point, Shackleton decided to risk a mountain crossing to the whaling station on the northern coast of South Georgia Island because of the wild storms on the sea and the damage to their makeshift sailboat. With no map or climbing equipment, and only boots jerry-rigged with screws to traverse the ice and steep terrain, the three men hiked 32 miles through the windswept and dangerous mountains without stopping, a climbing feat that was so difficult it was not accomplished by anyone else for almost another four decades. It was only when they reached the whaling station that they could truly breathe.

Immediately, Shackleton tried to send boats to the remaining twenty-two crew members on Elephant Island. After several unsuccessful attempts to reach Elephant Island, which was surrounded by moving ice floes, it took until August 30, 1916, for the rest of the crew to be rescued by Shackleton and a small tug ship, the *Yelcho*, lent by the Chilean government.

Out of the initial *Endurance* crew members, no lives were lost, and they all got to go home—an epic tale of survival made primarily possible by Shackleton's Exploratory Leadership and the crew's skills. Shackleton's actions demonstrated how he switched roles from being the regimented boss of the crew to being a nimble leader figuring out how to survive. This allowed him to lead with the correct tools (mindset, competency, and method) at the right moments.

And that is how Shackleton brought his entire crew safely home.

Exploratory Principle 7: Navigate through Reflection

Reflection compounds learning. And when launching ideas in the Realm of the Unknown, you need to manage survival and explore new ways to provide value.

Just like music, the structures of our activities flow in a pattern of tension and release. Tension is when we are engaged in our work; release comes when we have achieved our goal and stop our activities to rest and reflect. And then we gear up again for our next activities, and so the cycle goes. It is easy to see this pattern when the activity has discrete beginnings and endings, such as mounting an expedition to Antarctica, building a house, or acting in a play at the community theater. The finale always calls for a bit of celebration and letting loose. But when your schedule is a nine-to-five job or 24/7 eyes on your business, the release needs to be intentional or it won't happen. For just as in music, you must resolve the tension or people will be unhappy. And that's exactly why we have walks in the woods, happy hours, and evening classes for people who work nine to five.

One man who harks back to the past for the sake of the future is Kevin Cashman, author of *The Pause Principle: Step Back to Lead Forward*. Cashman says, "Leaders, especially, when faced with complexity and ambiguity, need to pause and 'slow the picture down' to see multiple options, multiple futures more effectively."

It is important to build time for reflection into our downtime, for it too is part of the life cycle of our exploratory activity. It ought to be in Ecclesiastes: There is a time to engage, and a time to reflect. To everything there is a season.

Exploratory leaders have rhythm. So don't let your phone or computer consume all of your downtime! Typically, those devices just cause more tension rather than release.

You can cover various topics in your reflections, and you can go about it in different ways. One key design element is that reflection should be conducted in a relaxed setting where your mind can flow, such as sitting in a chair, jogging on a path, or (like us when we launched Studio/E) hiking through the mountains. The key is intention. When we think about our work or explorations from a relaxed perspective, we see things in a different way. We can assess and learn where to aim our energies more productively. We can check in to see if we're aligned with our purpose and taking the right action steps with our possibilities. For most people, this means not trying to force their own thoughts. Rather, allow thoughts to emerge in bits and pieces. The point is, if we force our learning, we're likely to learn exactly what we expect. But if we can stay in that wonderful curious explorer's mindset during our reflections, it's quite likely that we'll connect some important dots as our ideas come into greater and greater form and clarity.

We can use our energies all week long as productively as we can, and then periodically we put down our work and reflect on the meaning of it and its impact. Perhaps we can learn what we can do better in the next iteration. Otherwise, we are just in reactive mode where events or others shape our destiny.

Many are intelligent, but few are wise. Wisdom comes from experience and reflection. Reflection is like compound interest. Our learning builds upon itself and ferments, so it ripens into wisdom over time. Reflection creates compound learning, which in turn generates deep confidence.

Taking action is like firing a weapon. Reflection is like aiming. In other words, without reflection, it's quite likely that you will either miss your targets or hit them inconsistently. Or in some cases you will hit the wrong target with amazing accuracy.

There are many modes of reflection, including journaling, keeping a logbook of what is happening on your journey, meditating, taking a walk, talking with another, and practicing breath work, to name a few. Journaling is one of our favorites. Putting down our words and ideas is an ancient principle and one that we highly recommend to all. Even if you are journaling minimally, it is valuable whenever you pause, think deeply, and archive what comes to mind.

Whether you fill pages upon pages or scribble out a few thoughts or even make a drawing of what's on your mind, what matters most is how often you engage in this important activity. Find a comfy place, commit to a regular cadence, and enjoy the rhythm. Your consistency will be rewarded because of this: Ideas flow in bits and pieces.

Yes, it would be so lovely and convenient if our ideas emerged as well-formed concepts as concise as the axioms of symbolic logic. Unfortunately, that's rarely the case. Consistent journaling or any form of reflection will allow you to review your past thoughts and piece them together to create new *current means*.

Sit back, breathe deeply, and ponder: What event is happening at this moment, and what does it mean for the steps you might take ahead? If you commit to reflection, valuable insights will show up, allowing you to confidently see more possibility to explore next.

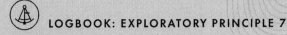

NAVIGATE THROUGH REFLECTION

Lesson

Reflection compounds learning. Remember, when you regularly reflect and build upon what you have experienced over time, your learnings become wisdom, and that generates confidence.

Question

Upon reflection, what is your next step?

_____

_____

_____

_____

_____

_____

_____

_____

Practice

After completing the declared action for your idea MVP, answer the following reflection questions.

Reflection Questions for Completed Idea MVP:

* **Learning:** What did you learn?

* **Possibility:** What is possible if you embrace this learning?

* **Consequences:** What are the consequences if you don't embrace this learning?

* **Action:** What action are you going to take next?

Example

Completed idea MVP: Create a run of show for beta day.

* **Learning:** People I have shared the run of show with are very engaged and supportive. The run of show I had envisioned had way too much in it for a single beta day. Everyone who is invited to beta day should know it's a beta day.

* **Possibility:** We could create a program that would help thousands of leaders courageously explore the unknown to discover more possibility.

* **Consequences:** We would be focused on perfection and delay or never launch anything, and the idea could end on the drafting table.

* **Action:** Our next MVPs will be to enroll fifteen participants for beta day and to decide on a date and location.

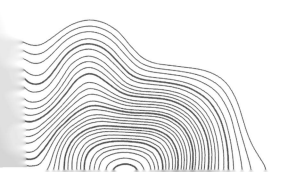

PART THREE

PLANT YOUR FLAG

The principles of Exploratory Leadership will equip you to launch new journeys into the unknown that will allow you to discover more possibilities to create the future you desire.

THIS IS not the ending, it's a beginning.

We are all born to be explorers. Once a baby can crawl, the expedition is launched. Driven by curiosity about everything, the baby explorer confronts new possibilities and new wonders every second. Some discoveries are delightful and make them laugh; others are terrifying and make them cry. Every new day is an adventure, filled with awe and wonder. As soon as they can talk, they become singers; when they can walk, they become dancers; and once they can grab a crayon, they become artists. Any stray object can become a toy. Anything that can fit into their mouths is possible food. Their imaginations run rampant, their actions are spontaneous, and almost anything seems possible. We need to re-awaken that exploratory way of being.

Exploratory Leadership Principles can be effectively used to explore, launch, and navigate any idea expedition into the unknown, as well as any challenge, issue, or even crisis. This method works personally and professionally, and the principles can be used individually or collectively to successfully navigate our rapidly changing world.

Understanding the ideas presented in the principles of becoming an exploratory leader is not the same thing as knowing how to *be* such a leader.

Knowing how to be a leader only comes through action, practice, more practice, and then some. The mastery of any activity entails practicing techniques to such an extent that they become automatic, and this frees your mind to focus on the objective. If this book had been about how to ride a bicycle, you would understand the theory all right, but you wouldn't know how to ride a bike until you actually got on one and practiced the art of balancing on two wheels, feeling how acceleration smooths out wobbliness, and mastering the variations of riding on dry pavement, slick roads, and muddy paths. Only experience can teach you the nuances.

In fact, we often believe that we either grow or decline. It is the biology of life.

The illusion that the status quo is safe leads down a false path. If you want to learn, and learn fast, move a few steps outside of your comfort zone and trek into the great unknown with a new method and tools. Take a breath. Here is where the adventure begins! Exploring the unknown leads to deep learning, relevance, and possibility. Those outcomes lead to new thinking, transformation, and innovation.

An exploratory leader masters the art of motivating people (including themselves) to effectively travel into the unknown with clarity and confidence to discover more possibility. The outcome of this type of leadership is creating more opportunities for you and your team so you can build more prosperous pathways in a world that is remaking itself over and over again every day.

Mastering a computer keyboard means that your fingers know by themselves how to find the right keys; all you need to focus on is what you want to type. The master violinist practices scales endlessly so that she simply needs to think of the sound she wants, and her fingers automatically find the right spot on the right string with the right vibrato. Once the techniques become habitual, the master violinist can focus on the only thing that matters: interpreting the music in a way that uplifts the audience with joy and shining eyes.

Let's review the principles that you need to master to become a practicing exploratory leader:

Principle 1: Explore in alignment with your purpose.

Principle 2: Launch with a curious explorer's mindset.

Principle 3: Launch with an exploratory learning community.

Principle 4: Navigate with packaged idea MVPs.

Principle 5: Navigate with exploratory questions.

Principle 6: Navigate with declared action.

Principle 7: Navigate through reflection.

Over time, as you consistently practice these principles, they will become automatic, so that your mind is free to engage in the discovery of new possibilities as you conduct your idea expeditions into the unknown. As we have said before, you can use these principles individually or collectively. Don't wait for perfection and think that it's only after the techniques become habitual and ingrained that you are ready to embark on your own expedition. The time is now!

To help you plant your flag on your idea expeditions, we invented a simple tool called the Expedition Action Compass that brings together all 7 Exploratory Leadership Principles in one place. To this point, we have been explaining the Expedition Map so you have context for the terrain ahead. However, philosopher and engineer Alfred Korzybski wisely pointed out, "A map is not the territory it represents," meaning we should not confuse a map with reality itself. You still need to explore the unknown territory and determine what is really going on. For example, the ice floes Shackleton faced so early in his expedition were not on the map. You will go on many idea expeditions into the unknown and face unexpected obstacles along the way. To aid in those expeditions and deal with those obstacles, we have included the Expedition Action Compass in Appendix B.

When using a map to navigate, you use a compass to find the intended direction of travel. Just as a regular compass points to the North Magnetic Pole, the Expedition Action Compass points to your magnetic north, fueled by your purpose. The Expedition Action Compass will get your idea expedition into motion by helping you identify the action you should take. Once you move forward with the Expedition Action Compass, complete your idea MVP, and reflect on it, you then create a new Expedition Action Compass to keep going in the unknown. You keep identifying, taking action, reflecting on idea MVPs, and launching new MVPs until your idea is launched—or you decide to kill it! Countless exploratory leaders have used the Expedition Action Compass or its principles for more than a decade to successfully explore, launch new ideas, navigate change, and plant their flags. We hope you will join those ranks and plant your flag.

The more you try, the better and better you will become at achieving this powerful way of behaving in the face of the unprecedented challenges of our world. Once you have launched, the trick is to also navigate the unknown with the attitude that "better" beats "perfect." In fact, better beats perfect almost all the time. Rather than assume you can design the perfect approach and launch an entire idea with exacting success, reflect on the smaller steps (idea MVPs) you have taken, and measure your progress (metrics) in the unknown.

The principles of Exploratory Leadership will equip you to launch new journeys into the unknown that will allow you to discover more possibilities to create the future you desire.

To put the principles in a clearer perspective, exploratory leaders participate, operate with dual literacy (awareness of the known and unknown), and . . .

- **explore** in alignment with their purpose;

- **launch** using a curious explorer's mindset within an exploratory learning community; and

- **navigate** with packaged idea MVPs, exploratory questions, declared action, and reflection.

Now go forth: Explore, launch, navigate, and create a more prosperous future for yourself, your teams, and the communities that support you.

May you live a truthful life and help others do the same. May you create civic health and make the world a better place. May you overlap your purpose with ours and go create more possibility and the future you desire.

Bon voyage!

ACKNOWLEDGMENTS

WE WOULD like to thank our awesome wives, Janine Brown and Trissa Garvis, for their unwavering support and for encouraging us to explore, launch, and navigate the Studio/E Expedition Program.

To do great things in this world requires a great team. We owe a huge debt of gratitude to our book team: Steve LeBeau, Kolina Cicero, Stiles Anderson, Peter Bailey, Jeff Johnson, and the crew at Page Two.

Steve is a cherished member of the Studio/E community, but beyond that he's an extremely gifted writer whose assistance was instrumental in crafting the voice, structure, and overall flow of this book.

Kolina was with Studio/E when it was just an idea. Thanks to Kolina and her great writing skills, we were able to gather our thoughts and get them down on paper to get this project moving.

Stiles helped bring this project home, always giving us the gift of his wise counsel, logic, personal experiences as a great exploratory practitioner, and extreme doses of patience.

Peter joined us in the very beginning helping us design and guide our Studio/E Expedition Program for more than a decade. He is a gifted exploratory leader and wise soul, and we are grateful for his contributions and boundless energy.

Jeff and his firm, Replace, designed our tools and symbols.

The crew at Page Two took our first edition and made it even better! A special thanks to Jesse Finkelstein, Caela Moffet, James Harbeck, Lisa Thomas-Tench, Jenny Govier, Peter Cocking, and Fiona Lee for their professional guidance, coaching, and expertise.

Our book team made this dream a reality, and we are extremely grateful for their help.

Studio/E has been an amazing adventure. What started as an idea during a walk in Aspen, Colorado, has turned into a world-class experience shared by thousands of leaders from every walk of life. As with all great creations, amazing souls have emerged to help us navigate the terrain of making this dream a reality.

A special shout-out to Heidi Neck and Cheryl Yaffe Kiser, who helped us give birth to the initial thinking that became Studio/E. We are incredibly grateful for these two wonderful women. Before there was a Studio/E, the four of us (self-described as Team Zodiac) hunkered down at Babson College with a dream. Heidi and Cheryl helped create the spark that still burns and put us on a trajectory that we honor to this day. They are magical and brilliant souls.

We thank the following who also helped us with this journey: Simone Ahuja, Ryan Baum, Christine Bent,

Beth Biersdorf, Terry Clark, Jackie Colburn, Cristina Corrie, Julie Engel, Erik Gabrielson, Bob Gardner, Pilar Gerasimo, Jackie Gibney, Julie Guggemos, Lori Hall, Jared Hanks, Rob Holt, Greg Heinemann, Katie Jauert, Bruce King-Shey, Jodee Kozlak, Vikas Narula, Rhoda Olsen, Dev Patnaik, Ken Paulus, Tawnee Rebhuhn, Jill Sando, Len Schlesinger, Linda Schwefel, Scott Schwefel, Tessa Tangney, Stephanie Unterberger, Todd Waterbury, Jackson Wiese, Shaefer Wiese, Andrew Zimmern, and everyone who graced us by participating in the many Studio/E experiences produced over the years.

Thanks also to our collaborators along the way: Activ8, Babson College's Institute for Social Innovation, Blood Orange, GoKart Labs (now part of West Monroe), Green Mangos Catering & Team, James J. Hill Center, Jump, Keyhubs, Latitude, Mayfly Design, Minneapolis Institute of Art, Prouty Project, Replace, Room 34, Scout Workshop, Sprint!, and Voyageur Outward Bound.

APPENDIX A: EXPEDITION MAP

REFLECTION

UNKNOWN

Navigate

STUDIO/E METHOD

Launch

POSSIBILITY

Explore

PREDICTION

AWARENESS & CHOICE

KNOWN

EXPEDITION ACTION COMPASS—WORKSHEET

1. Purpose Sentence

_____

_____

2. Mindset

Three curious-explorer's-mindset words/curious-explorer story

_____ _____ _____

_____

_____

_____

3. Exploratory Learning Community

_____

_____

4. Packaged Idea MVP

Idea Name: _____

_____ -Day Idea MVP: _____
[A step that will move your idea forward.]

Metric(s) for Idea MVP: _____

_____

5. Exploratory Questions

6. Declared Action (noun, verb, date)

Current Means: What do you have to put toward your idea right now?

Experiences:
Skills:
Relationships:

Ideation: What makes your idea of unique value to its users?

Boundaries: What are you willing to invest (and not invest) in your idea to take the next step?

Enrollment: Who can make your idea better, and why would they help?

7. Reflection on the Declared Action for Your Idea MVP upon Its Completion

What did you learn?

_____

What is possible if you embrace this learning?

_____

What are the consequences if you don't embrace this learning?

_____

What action are you going to take next?

_____

Note: Upon completion of your reflection, repeat Principles 4 to 7 for your next idea MVPs until your idea is launched— or you decide to kill it!

Go to **exploreorexpirebook.com** for printable worksheets and additional examples of completed worksheets.

EXPEDITION ACTION COMPASS—WORKSHEET

1. Purpose Sentence

My purpose is to share the wisdom of others to help people discover more possibility.

2. Mindset

Three curious-explorer's-mindset words/curious-explorer story

Curiosity, generosity, growth

My curiosity and generosity are huge assets for discovering how I can help others think differently and launch new ideas.

3. Exploratory Learning Community

I will recruit and enroll Kevin (teacher), Rip (writer), and Lani (leadership development expert), and we will help each other navigate our challenges and celebrate our successes.

4. Packaged Idea MVP

Idea Name: *Expedition Program*

30 -**Day Idea MVP:** *Create a run of show for beta day.*

Metric(s) for Idea MVP: *Identify at least seven content modules in the run of show.*

5. Exploratory Questions

 ## 6. Declared Action (noun, verb, date)

Current Means: What do you have to put toward your idea right now?

Experiences: *Attended great leadership programs and coached teams.*

I will design a run of show (draft 1) for beta day loosely based on (not copying) the formats I have from other leadership programs within the next four days.

Skills: *Have done public speaking and provided counsel for leaders.*

Relationships: *Worked with many thought leaders, corporate leaders, teachers, and entrepreneurs.*

Ideation: What makes your idea of unique value to its users?

I will include a story of a courageous explorer within the content of the run of show within the next seven days.

This idea will inspire leaders and their teams to courageously explore unknown realms to discover more possibility.

5. Exploratory Questions

6. Declared Action (noun, verb, date)

Boundaries: What are you willing to invest (and not invest) in your idea to take the next step?

Time: *10 to 20 hours*
Money: *$0 to $100 for lunches*

I will share run of show with two thought leaders in the leadership development space for feedback. I will not share this with potential sponsors until later.

I will finalize the run of show so that it can be shared for feedback with thought leaders in the next fourteen days.

Enrollment: Who can make your idea better, and why would they help?

I will enroll two thought leaders, Cheryl and Heidi, as they have created many successful programs and are interested in exploration to help others grow.

I will share the run of show with two thought leaders, Cheryl and Heidi, and incorporate their overall feedback, and I will have at least seven content modules within the next thirty days.

7. Reflection on the Declared Action for Your Idea MVP upon Its Completion

What did you learn? *People I have shared the run of show with are very engaged and supportive. The run of show I had envisioned had way too much in it for a single beta day. Everyone who is invited to beta day should know it's a beta day.*

What is possible if you embrace this learning? *We could create a program that would help thousands of leaders courageously explore the unknown to discover more possibility.*

What are the consequences if you don't embrace this learning? *We would be focused on perfection and delay or never launch anything, and the idea could end on the drafting table.*

What action are you going to take next? *Our next MVPs will be to enroll fifteen participants for beta day and to decide on a date and location.*

INSPIRATIONS

BELOW ARE some of our favorite exploratory leaders (and the list keeps growing). Many of these Hero Teachers have shared their wisdom directly with Studio/E via presentations and interviews in recent years. We encourage you to check them out. The Reading List that follows includes books written by and biographies about many of these Hero Teachers.

Peter Bailey, experiential designer, facilitator

Dr. Harold Brown, Tuskegee airman, educator

Michael Bungay Stanier, coach, speaker

Jimmy Chin, award-winning filmmaker, mountain sports athlete

Lynne Cox, long-distance open-water swimmer, peace builder

Greg Cunningham, senior executive VP and chief diversity officer, storyteller

Jessie Diggins, American cross-country skier, Olympic gold medalist

Jenny Evans, coach, resiliency expert

Ron Finley, gardener, artist, teacher

Tyler Fish, first American to ski unassisted to the North Pole (with John Huston), coach

Erik Gabrielson, igniter, performance coach

Pilar Gerasimo, health journalist, coach, illustrator

Phil Hansen, multimedia artist

Ryan Holiday, marketer, entrepreneur

David Horsager, researcher, trust expert

Guy Kawasaki, podcaster, father of Brand Evangelism

Ingrid Fetell Lee, designer, joy evangelist

Dr. Kelly McGonigal, psychologist, teacher

Greg McKeown, essentialist, teacher

John O'Leary, inspirational speaker, podcaster

Priya Parker, master convener, dispute resolution artist

Dan Roam, visual communicator, clarity expert

Len Schlesinger, business leader, educator, former college president

Sir Ernest Shackleton, Antarctic explorer

Cecily Sommers, futurist, innovation expert

David and Jonah Stillman, father/son generational experts and teachers

Christina Tosi, chef, entrepreneur

Terry Wu, PhD, neuroscientist, marketing consultant

Benjamin Zander, musician, conductor, educator

Andrew Zimmern, chef, TV personality, producer

READING LIST

Alexander, Caroline. *The Endurance: Shackleton's Legendary Antarctic Expedition.* Reprint. New York: Alfred A. Knopf, Inc., 2001.

The Arbinger Institute. *The Outward Mindset: How to Change Lives and Transform Organizations.* Oakland, CA: Berrett-Koehler Publishers, 2019.

Berger, Warren. *A More Beautiful Question: The Power of Inquiry to Seek Breakthrough Ideas.* New York: Bloomsbury, 2014.

Boynton, Andy, and Bill Fischer. *The Idea Hunter: How to Find the Best Ideas and Make Them Happen.* San Francisco: Jossey-Bass, 2011.

Brown, Harold H., and Marcia S. Bordner. *Keep Your Airspeed Up: The Story of a Tuskegee Airman.* Tuscaloosa, AL: University of Alabama Press, 2017.

Bungay Stanier, Michael. "I'm Scarred." In *End Malaria: Bold Innovation, Limitless Generosity, and the Opportunity to Save a Life*, edited by Michael Bungay Stanier. Domino Project, 2011.

Bungay Stanier, Michael. *The Coaching Habit: Say Less, Ask More & Change the Way You Lead Forever.* Toronto: Box of Crayons Press, 2016.

Cashman, Kevin. *The Pause Principle: Step Back to Lead Forward*. San Francisco: Berrett-Koehler Publishers, 2012.

Collins, Jim, and Morten T. Hansen. *Great by Choice: Uncertainty, Chaos, and Luck—Why Some Thrive Despite Them All*. New York: Harper Business, 2011.

Cramer, Kathryn, and Hank Wasiak. *Change the Way You See Everything through Asset-Based Thinking*. Philadelphia: Running Press, 2006.

Dweck, Carol S. *Mindset: The New Psychology of Success*. Revised edition. New York: Random House, 2016.

Frankl, Viktor E. *Man's Search for Meaning*. Translated by Ilse Lasch. Boston: Beacon Press, 2006.

George, Bill, and Doug Baker. *True North Groups: A Powerful Path to Personal and Leadership Development*. Oakland, CA: Berrett-Koehler Publishers, 2011.

Godin, Seth. *What to Do When It's Your Turn (And It's Always Your Turn)*. Domino Project, 2020.

Goldsmith, Marshall, and Mark Reiter. *Triggers: Creating Behavior That Lasts—Becoming the Person You Want to Be*. New York: Crown Business, 2015.

Heffernan, Margaret. *Uncharted: How to Navigate the Future*. New York: Avid Read, 2020.

Hill, Napoleon. *Think and Grow Rich*. Revised and expanded by Arthur R. Pell. New York: Jeremy P. Tarcher/Penguin, 2005.

Holiday, Ryan. *The Obstacle Is the Way: The Timeless Art of Turning Trials into Triumph*. New York: Portfolio/Penguin, 2014.

Holiday, Ryan. *Perennial Seller: The Art of Making and Marketing Work That Lasts.* New York: Portfolio/ Penguin, 2017.

Holiday, Ryan. *Stillness Is the Key: An Ancient Strategy for Modern Life.* New York: Portfolio/Penguin, 2019.

Johnson, Steven. *Where Good Ideas Come From: The Natural History of Innovation.* New York: Riverhead Books, 2010.

Leider, Richard. *The Power of Purpose: Find Meaning, Live Longer, Better.* 3rd ed. Oakland, CA: Berrett-Koehler Publishers, 2015.

McKeown, Greg. *Essentialism: The Disciplined Pursuit of Less.* New York: Currency, 2020.

McNally, David. *Mark of an Eagle: How Your Life Changes the World.* Minneapolis: Wisdom Editions, 2017.

Morrell, Margot, and Stephanie Capparell. *Shackleton's Way: Leadership Lessons from the Great Antarctic Explorer.* New York: Penguin Books, 2001.

Neal, Craig, and Patricia Neal, with Cynthia Wold. *The Art of Convening: Authentic Engagement in Meetings, Gatherings, and Conversations.* Oakland, CA: Berrett-Koehler Publishers, 2011.

Osterwalder, Alexander, and Yves Pigneur. *Business Model Generation: A Handbook for Visionaries, Game Changers, and Challengers.* Hoboken, NJ: John Wiley & Sons, 2010.

Parker, Priya. *Art of Gathering: How We Meet and Why It Matters.* New York: Riverhead Books, 2018.

Pink, Daniel. *Drive: The Surprising Truth about What Motivates Us.* New York: Riverhead Books, 2011.

Pink, Daniel. *To Sell Is Human: The Surprising Truth about Moving Others.* New York: Riverhead Books, 2012.

Ries, Eric. *The Lean Startup: How Today's Entrepreneurs Use Continuous Innovation to Create Radically Successful Businesses.* New York: Currency, 2011.

Roam, Dan. *Draw to Win: A Crash Course on How to Lead, Sell, and Innovate with Your Visual Mind.* New York: Portfolio/Penguin, 2016.

Roberts, Kevin. *64 Shots: Leadership in a Crazy World.* New York: Powerhouse Books, 2016.

Schlesinger, Leonard A., and Charles F. Kiefer, with Paul B. Brown. *Just Start: Take Action, Embrace Uncertainty, Create the Future.* Boston: Harvard Business Review Press, 2012.

Simmons, Michael. "The No. 1 Predictor of Career Success According to Network Science." *Forbes,* January 16, 2016. (Discussing interview with Ronald S. Burt, Charles M. Harper Leadership Professor of Sociology and Strategy at the University of Chicago Booth School of Business.)

Sturridge, Charles, dir. *Shackleton: The Greatest Survival Story of All Time.* First broadcast in the US April 9, 2002, on A&E.

Young, James Webb. *A Technique for Producing Ideas.* New York: McGraw-Hill, 2003.

Zander, Benjamin, and Rosamund Stone Zander. *The Art of Possibility: Transforming Professional and Personal Life.* Revised edition. New York: Penguin Books, 2002.

ABOUT THE AUTHORS

Tom Wiese is an advisor and legal counsel to business leaders, a content and tool designer, a senior fellow at Babson College's Institute for Social Innovation and Social Innovation Lab, and a skier who shares in the great expedition of life with his wife and four children.

Nate Garvis is a civic designer and serves as strategic counsel to leaders across many sectors. He is a senior fellow at Babson College's Institute for Social Innovation and Social Innovation Lab, a former Fortune 50 public affairs executive, a musician, and an experienced global traveler who has used the planet and its people as a classroom for himself, his wife, and their two daughters.

Studio/E's purpose is to help leaders discover more possibility. Our belief is that exploration is essential to thriving in today's rapidly changing world. Our guiding principles empower leaders to *explore*, *launch*, and *navigate* new ideas that create pathways to accelerate value personally and professionally. Our services are provided through programming and guided exploratory learning communities.

Please visit our website at **exploreorexpirebook.com**.

Now go explore, launch, and navigate

Client to draw

G.MET Policy

Muscle/Images

- Brand Space

VP to conference

- GMET Htns

Trade Controls

- MMS

w/o 19.2
- 7

10/9 - 6.30

10/16 - 5

10/22 - 31

10/29 3/1
- 19

Made in the USA
Monee, IL
12 October 2023